Unleashing the Power of Food:

Recipes to Heal By

Published by Agora Health Books
819 North Charles Street • Baltimore, Maryland 21201

680CB0011

Unleashing the Power of Food : Recipes to Heal By

Second Edition

Published by Agora Health Books

Alice Jacob, Managing Editor

Ken Danz, Copy Editor

Additional orders and inquiries can be directed to Agora Health Books, Customer Service Department, 819 N. Charles Street, Baltimore, MD 21201; Tel: (203) 699-3697, Fax: (410) 230-1273, E-mail: ahb@agora-inc.com.

ISBN 1-891434-16-0

Printed in the United States of America

Agora Health Books
819 N. Charles Street
Baltimore, Maryland 21201
www.agorahealthbooks.com

Unleashing the Power of Food

Recipes to Heal By

by FaXiang Hou

Agora Health Books • Baltimore, Maryland

DISCLAIMER

All material in this publication is provided for information only and may not be construed as medical advice or instruction. No action or inaction should be taken based solely on the contents of this publication; instead, readers should consult appropriate health professionals on any matter relating to their health and well-being.

The information and opinions provided in this publication are believed to be accurate and sound, based on the best judgment available to the authors, but readers who fail to consult with appropriate health authorities assume the risk of any injuries. The publisher is not responsible for errors or omissions.

THE INFORMATION PRESENTED HERE HAS NOT BEEN EVALUATED BY THE U.S. FOOD & DRUG ADMINISTRATION. THIS PRODUCT IS NOT INTENDED TO DIAGNOSE, TREAT, CURE OR PREVENT ANY DISEASE.

Table of Contents

About Master FaXiang Hou

Master FaXiang Hou is a certified and highly accomplished Master of Medical QiGong therapy and Traditional Chinese Medicine. In the tradition of many great Masters, his methods of healing QiGong, acupuncture, and herbal medicine have been passed down through his family for five generations. He and his brother are the only known recipients of a unique and powerful form of healing QiGong called *Ching Loong San Dian Xue Mi Gong Fa*.

At the age of 13, Master Hou began training under his father in the healing arts. As a young adult, he continued his studies under five other accomplished Masters in China. He has undergone rigorous clinical testing of his healing ability in China and has had the rare honor of being deemed a Certified Master in the elite International Qigong Science Association, as well as the Chinese QiGong Association.

Master Hou has had great success treating a wide variety of chronic and acute ailments and diseases, including, to name just a few: chronic headaches and migraines, allergies, asthma, inflammatory conditions, insomnia, hypertension, intestinal inflammation, pneumonia, emphysema, arthritis, pleurisy, accidental injuries, edema, strains, sprains, dislocations, gynecological conditions, strokes, neurological disorders, blood disorders, non-metastasized cancers, vertebral conditions, chronic-fatigue syndrome, and the symptoms of HIV and AIDS.

Master Hou is currently the Director of The QiGong Research Society in Mount Laurel, New Jersey, and holds private consultations in Cherry Hill, New Jersey.

Introduction

When I was a younger man, contrary to my family teachings (and contrary even to the advice I was giving my own patients) I paid little attention to my personal diet and nutritional needs. I was healthy and in good physical condition and I didn't believe that a bad diet would affect me. I guess we all think we are immortal at that age. As I got older, however, I noticed that my physical health was starting to break down and I began to experience many of the same symptoms that my patients who were coming to see me for treatment were suffering from.

As I watched my health deteriorate I began to truly understand and appreciate the wisdom of my ancestors in a way I never had before. I truly connected with that ancient wisdom and I literally began to practice what I preached to my own patients.

As I embraced the teachings my family had passed along to me I became more concerned with my diet and I began to follow the ways of traditional Chinese longevity. I wanted to have a deeper understanding of the science behind my families teachings and in addition to my regular practice as an energy healer I spent four decades studying nutrition, the effects of food on the body, and Chinese cooking for health.

I feel it is vitally important to continue the tradition of sharing this healing wisdom with others. I carry out this obligation by passing on what I have learned to my patients and students with the hope that they will learn, as I did, to truly appreciate the nutritional value of food and the impact it has on our health. I try to help them identify what foods are right for them individually as well as the proper cooking methods for those foods.

Unfortunately, my time is very limited due to my growing healing practice and I can't personally counsel as many people as I would like. The idea to create this book, in fact, was born out of the need I feel to share my healing knowledge with as many people as I possibly can. Though I am neither a fancy chef nor a great writer, I decided to write this book so that you might understand the important role food plays in your health and so you can begin to make the right dietary choices to promote good health and healing in your own life.

"I feel it is vitally important to continue the tradition of sharing this healing wisdom with others."

We eat everyday in order to satisfy our hunger and quench our thirst. But the food we consume does so much more than this. Food actually acts as a kind of medicine. And unlike many of the mainstream medicines used to "cure" illnesses, food can actually prevent them from even gaining a foothold in the first place.

Oriental cooking, especially Chinese, is completely different from Western cooking in its background, materials, and methods. The traditional Chinese diet, with its emphasis on vegetables and plant proteins, serves as a powerful preventive against disease.

Indeed, the Chinese philosophy of food has much to offer the American palate and American health. Throughout their history, the Chinese have placed much emphasis on food as a means of maintaining health. In fact, as early as 2500 B.C., Chinese scholars had developed a systematic theory linking food to physical well-being. In China we believe that food works much like medicine. And though it may work more slowly than medicine, food plays a crucial role in illness prevention and long-term cures.

It has been proven time and again that, regardless of the particular illness involved, when patients take a proactive approach to their diet their diseases take a favorable turn. Sometimes this turn can be measured in as little as two weeks time. I personally have witnessed this transformation countless times in my own practice. With the proper food choices and preparation patients become physically stronger and their troubling symptoms begin to abate.

The Chinese believe that the spleen (known as pi in Chinese) and the stomach (called wei in Chinese) digest and absorb the nutritional elements in food. This belief holds that good health depends on keeping the spleen and stomach in good working condition and this is accomplished through the eating of proper foods. Food is essentially performing as a slow-acting all-natural medicine without the negative side effects that are often seen with harsher Western approaches.

The traditional Chinese diet consists mainly of plant foods and features low-fat, low-calorie, and high-fiber dishes. Any doctor, western or not, will tell you that the preceding sentence reads like a recipe for good health. And this intuitively healthy eating style is why China's rates of hypertension, diabetes, and obesity fall far short of those of those so-called *more-advanced* countries like the United States. Although, I am sad to say, that as the poor eating habits of the Western world have begun to invade China we are starting to see diet related diseases on the rise.

Interestingly, it is not only the *types* of foods that differ between East and West but the actual preparation of a traditional Chinese meal is also very different as well. In preparing meals, the Chinese purposefully try to combine complementary ingredients. We want to harmonize the ingredients to help prevent and relieve different conditions. Turnip, for example, is usually prepared with lamb or beef, as turnip is considered a "cool" food while lamb and beef are considered "warm" in nature. When you combine them, the heat within beef or lamb is greatly reduced by the turnip, therefore making the dish *calm* and thus healthier and easier to digest. In other words by balancing the foods within a meal you prevent imbalances in the body of the person eating the meal.

In **Unleashing the Power of Food** I have hand-picked traditional healing recipes that can be easily understood and prepared even by those who have never tried cooking a Chinese meal. In fact many of them require so little preparation that a child can easily be taught to prepare them with adult supervision. Still, a few may seem strange and somewhat awkward when you first attempt to make them. But don't let the seemingly exotic nature stop you from giving them a try. I assure you that you will be pleasantly surprised and your body will thank you.

Most of the recipes I have chosen for you have been

A TIP FROM THE MASTER

According to Traditional Chinese Medicine, good health depends on keeping the stomach and spleen in good working order.

Pi = spleen in Chinese

Wei = stomach in Chinese

in China for a very long time. Make no mistake, these recipes are not Americanized versions of Chinese food like so many Chinese food cookbooks offer. Some of them I picked because they are the Chinese-food answer to fast food: quick, easy to fix, economical, and tasty. Yet, unlike fast food burgers and fries, these dishes properly nourish your body and prevent illness and disease. I have included other recipes that are traditional dishes from the various regions in China. These recipes offer different taste sensations that will please your palate while they balance your body. Still others are designed for entertaining family and friends—meals intended for nourishing both relationships and bodies.

I personally use these recipes and I recommend them to my patients. They are carefully balanced to be both high in nutritional content and healing properties. To reap the most benefit from these recipes, I strongly urge you to choose only fresh, organic foods whenever possible.

Many of the ingredients called for in my recipes can easily be found in your local grocery or fresh food stores (try the international aisle) and some of the slightly less common ingredients can be purchased in almost any Asian market. There are some recipes that I have included in which some of the ingredients might be unfamiliar to you. For example some recipes call for items like lotus roots or asparagus lettuce. If you flipped through the book before you settled down to read it, you have probably have already noticed that throughout the book I have included little tidbits of helpful information labeled "A Tip From the Master". Many of these tips contain helpful information about the somewhat more exotic ingredients I call for in my recipes. If you are still stumped finding an ingredient ask at your local Asian food market. If they do not have the item on hand they probably can order it for you. If your having trouble locating an Asian market in your area stop by your favorite Chinese or Asian carry-out and ask them where they buy their ingredients. More than likely they will be happy to share this information with you.

Please keep in mind that food should never be *substituted* for medicine when a condition already exists. I don't want anyone to misunderstand the healing power of food alone. Medically speaking, food can only assist in the healing process. For example though carrots contain betacarotene, which is good for eyesight, you cannot heal cataracts simply by eating a bag of carrots. And, of course, you should never discontinue the use of prescription medications without discussing it with your physician first. The prevention of illness and maintenance of health rely on many factors. Food, though an extremely important factor, is only one of them.

"My suggestion for good health is very simple: engage in physical and mental exercise, select and combine the proper foods, and cook them in the correct way."

My suggestion for good health is very simple: engage in physical and mental exercise, select and combine the proper foods, and cook them in the correct way. By doing so, you can help prevent illness and greatly reduce or reverse those that already lurk within you.

This book is divided into two main sections. Part One, "Preliminaries," provides a quick and easy introduction to the Chinese medicine approach to food Part Two, "Chinese Recipes for Health," provides more than 200 of my most powerful personal curative recipes to help heal and prevent illness. I follow the recipes up with several helpful appendixes to help you personalize your new healthy approach to eating. Also, be sure to take a look at the resources section beginning on page 335. In this section I provide you with several reliable online sources for purchasing some of the Asian food items called for in my recipes as well as useful kitchen equipment like woks and steamers.

I included some helpful sample diet plans in Appendix III starting on page 312. Make sure to spend some time looking through these plans as they offer a detailed list of foods that you should be sure to eat and trigger foods that you should be avoiding to control or heal many common ailments. In addition I have included specific dietary approaches for dealing with hypertension, diabetes, obesity, heart disease, and cancer. You can use these plans as a basic guideline for creating personal dietary plans that incorporate my healing recipes to meet your own individual needs and tastes.

As you start cooking and eating healthy and your body becomes accustomed to a good diet you will find yourself naturally avoiding junk food and instinctively making the right food choices. And trust me it is a powerful feeling when you find yourself intuitively choosing what your body needs to be healthy and when you become in tune with your bodies changing needs when illness threatens your good health.

I would like to extend my thanks to Eric Yin, who helped me to collect and translate all the materials for this book and to Agora Health Books for their enthusiasm in this project and willingness to publish it.

– Master FaXiang Hou
Mount Laurel, New Jersey

PART ONE
PRELIMINARIES

CHAPTER I

We Are What We Eat

Few Westerners truly consider the connection between food and health. This should not be seen as a fault, but rather simply a fact borne out of a culture that does not encourage such thinking. Sure, we hear news stories every day that report on studies that draw a seemingly unmistakable connection between what we eat and the steadily declining state of our health here in the West. Yet for most of us no real connection is made between what we put in our mouths and the state of our health.

High calorie foods with low nutritional value make up a large part of the typical Western diet. In fact one study, published in the *American Journal of Clinical Nutrition,* found that a full 31% of the average American's total calorie consumption is coming from snack foods, alcohol, and condiments. The third edition of the *National Health and Nutritional Examination Survey* took a look at the eating patterns of fifteen thousand American adults and it was determined that 27 percent of their total caloric intake was coming from "junk food" (foods that do not fall within the five major food groups)

"Food has the power to poison or strengthen our bodies."

and another 4 percent of their calories were coming from alcohol.

While food might not have much of an impact on our thoughts it does have an undeniable effect on our health. As the consumption of junk foods and processed sugars continues to rise so do the numbers of Americans suffering from obesity, heart disease, hypertension, diabetes, and cancer. Food has the power to poison or strengthen our bodies. The foods you eat can operate in your system like a weight upon your body causing fatigue, illness, and even disease or it can power you to an advanced level of good health allowing you to enjoy energy filled days and a long life. Like medicine, the proper foods can help cure many illnesses. A relatively simple change in diet can often alter or even halt a disease process. By choosing the right foods, we can restore our energy, vitality, and good health.

Western doctors prescribe medications in reaction to the illnesses that their patients suffer from. The medicines are used to cure or treat existing diseases. Few physicians realize that carefully selected foods can be used medicinally to heal or treat the sick as well. Even fewer doctors understand that foods have a healing energy that goes well beyond the scope of traditional Western medicine. By eating the right foods in the right combinations, we have the power to prevent disease and illness from ever occurring.

The Chinese have understood this connection between food and illness for thousands of years. The concept that what we eat directly influences how we feel is a basic building block of Chinese medicine. Indeed, the Chinese concept of balanced nutrition has much to teach the West. Food is selected and prepared according to specific guidelines that allow the natural ability of foods to prevent and heal illness to be harnessed for our own benefit. The success of these dietary techniques is illustrated in the many centuries of vibrant health that the Chinese have enjoyed—health that is now being threatened as the eating habits of the Western world are being adopted by the younger generation in China.

Few people would question that certain kinds of foods can be a factor in illnesses, including hypertension, coronary heart disease, diabetes, and ulcers. We need look no further than the typical American high-fat animal-based diet for an illustration of the effect that food can have on health. In fact, Americans generally get about a third of their

A TIP FROM THE MASTER

To determine how healthy a certain food is quickly and easily access how plain it is. Less processing means the food is closer to its pure and natural state and is healthier for you.

A TIP FROM THE MASTER

Unfortunately, Americanized versions of traditional Asian foods are often pale imitations of the real thing containing too much salt, sugar, fat, and meat. When eating Asian food in a restuarant it is often best to choose vegetarian dishes and specifically ask that sugar and salt not be added to your meal. Since the majority of Asian dishes are made to order most restaurants will happily comply with your special requests.

---

daily caloric intake from animal-based foods, and animal protein makes up 70 percent of their total protein intake. The effects of this ill-advised diet are illustrated by the dramatic rise in diet-related diseases in the West including obesity, hypertension, heart disease, and diabetes.

Just as eating the wrong foods can lead to illness, eating the right ones can lead to good health. The simplest guide for determining how healthy a food is to access how *plain* it is. Less processing means the food is closer to its pure and natural state and is better for you. In other words the more basic or pure a food is, the less processing it has gone through, the healthier it is for you. Traditionally, the Chinese daily diet is made up of plain foods like grains and vegetables. Many of the diseases plaguing the Western World are virtually nonexistent in China (although the tide appears to be changing as poor Western eating habits are being adopted by young Chinese men and women).

The Chinese identified the connection between food and illness long ago. There are dozens of ancient books in China dedicated to dietary concerns and proper eating habits. Some of these basic common-sense guidelines have remained essentially unchanged for centuries, such as understanding the benefits of eating meals at regular times, curbing overeating, and avoiding eating only one type of food.

"You have the power to control your health and how you feel by what you choose to put into your mouth."

Over 2000 years ago the Chinese text *Lushi Chunquin* drew a clear connection between food and health when it warned, "thick and pungent tastes are the incentives of illness." The early healers of the text warned against greasy, deep-fried, and pungent foods saying they could "promote the production of phlegm and create dumpiness; raise liver's yang and invite liver's wind." It's as good advice today as it was 2000 years ago.

Despite the fact that the health benefits of a plant-based diet are already well understood in the West, this knowledge seems rarely put into practical use by Americans. I urge my patients, and all Westerners, to try to think more like the Chinese do about food. There is validity in that old saying "You are what you eat". Like most old sayings it is rooted firmly in the truth. Food can poison our bodies or lead us to perfect health. You have the power to control your health and how you feel by what you choose to put into your mouth. The choice is yours. Will you choose health, vitality, and longevity over illness, fatigue, and an early death?

CHAPTER 2

An Introduction to Traditional Chinese Medicine

Some of the concepts I will discuss in this chapter may, at first, seem foreign or challenging to you. However, these beliefs are far simpler than you might at first glance imagine them to be and they are fundamental to the secrets of Chinese health and longevity. With an understanding of these basic concepts you will begin to see the connection between food and health in a way you probably have never seen it before.

In Traditional Chinese Medicine (TCM), the individual is seen as part of a bigger picture—a piece of the natural universe. The theories that follow illustrate the belief that we are, just as the universe is, controlled by certain irrefutable rules of nature. The Chinese believe that the body, like the rest of nature, can be understood, and even manipulated, once this *framework* defining the natural world is understood. As you read through this book, you should begin to understand how these concepts work hand in hand with the food guidelines and recipes I have provided here for you. This new understanding will empower you to take control of your own health

A TIP FROM THE MASTER

Traditional Chinese Medicine is based on the balance between the two basic and opposite factors that make up everything in the universe known as yin (negative or passive elements) and yang (positive or active elements).

and well-being.

Yin and Yang Balance in the Body

A large emphasis is placed on the concept of balance in TCM. In fact the Chinese view the whole of the universe in terms of a balance between the two factors of yin (negative or passive elements) and yang (positive or active elements). The theory of yin and yang holds that all things have an opposite yet complementary aspect. It is important however, to understand that these two equal but opposite sides should never be thought of in terms of a Western sense of positive and negative (in other words good and bad). No judgment is attached to the opposite but equal aspects of yin and yang. Rather, it should be understood that they are dependent on each other for their very existence. After all, there is no hot without cold, no joy without sorrow, and no play without work. Thus, the balance between yin and yang represents a universal law of the material world. While these two aspects **are** in opposition to each other, because one end of the spectrum cannot exist without the other, they are also **dependent** on each other. The words yin and yang truly describe a character more than anything strictly material. Yin is best represented symbolically by things like water, quiet, substance, and night. While yang would be best represented as fire, noise, function, and day.

The human body is, as are all things in the universe, a balance of yin and yang. In Chinese medicine, it is taught that the body's five main organs—the heart, lungs, kidneys, liver, and spleen—regulate and control the body's major functions and its general health. The Chinese call these five main organs the *zang fu* or solid organs. In TCM these organs are given a great deal more power and responsibility than Western science assigns to them. All remaining organs are secondary to them and largely controlled by them.

The energy flow among the five zang-fu organs controls the delicate yin and yang balance of the body. Each of the solid organs of the body contains an element of yin and an element of yang. Some organs contain more yang, others more yin. In the healthy body, the yin and yang properties within are constantly fluctuating yet remain in continual balance with each other. When yin and yang go out of balance in a body, poor health generally follows. To restore your body to good health, you need to ensure that your body is returned to a balanced

A TIP FROM THE MASTER

In traditional Chinese Medicine the body is regulated and controlled by five main organs—the heart, the lungs, the kidneys, the liver, and the spleen—known as the zang fu or solid organs.

state. You can achieve this state of balance for your body through choosing the right foods and preparing them in the right manner.

In winter, for example, a practitioner of Chinese medicine would suggest eating more nutritionally dense foods. Much energy has been expended during the prior three seasons and replenishing the body during the winter months will restore balance. Also, the lower temperatures in winter mean that to maintain balance, and to keep the body warm, you must consume more calories.

In Chinese medicine we are taught that after food leaves the stomach the elements of that food are directed to certain organs based on the taste value of the particular food; sour foods go to the liver, bitter foods go to the heart, sweet foods go to the spleen, pungent foods go to the lungs, and salty foods go to the kidneys. With an understanding of this basic theory it becomes clear how diet can disrupt the yin and yang balance among the organs of the body. The five "tastes" should be coordinated, and one's diet should not be heavily biased toward any one taste at the expense of others. In short, a balance of yin and yang through proper selection, combining, and preparation of food is crucial to maintaining

A TIP FROM THE MASTER

In Traditional Chinese Medicine foods are assigned a taste value. Based on that taste value it is thought that the elements of that food are directed to specific organs. Below is a simple chart illustrating the relationship between the taste values of food and the organs.

Taste value	***Organ***
sour	*liver*
bitter	*heart*
sweet	*spleen*
pungent	*lungs*
salty	*kidney*

optimal health.

The Five-elements Theory

The five-elements theory explains the connection between the zang-fu organs I mentioned earlier and the body, as well as the relationship between the body and nature. The five elements refer to five categories of material found in the natural world: wood, fire, earth, metal, and water. The theory of the five elements holds that all phenomena in the universe correspond in nature to one of these materials and that they are in a state of constant motion and change as they interact with one another.

The theory of the five elements was formed in China at about the time of the Yin and Zhou dynasties (16th century-221 B.C.). Historically, the theory was derived from observations of the natural world made by the Chinese people in the course of their daily lives.

Wood, fire, earth, metal, and water were considered to be indispensable materials for maintaining a productive life. It was also understood that these elements were important to initiating normal changes in the natural world.

Each of the five zang-fu organs can be con-

A TIP FROM THE MASTER

In Traditional Chinese Medicine all phenomena in the universe can be tied to five basic elements found in nature; wood, fire, earth, metal, and water. Each of the zang fu organs discussed earlier can be connected to one of these five elements. The chart below illustrates this relationship.

Zang Fu Organ : Element Action/Role
liver : wood *regulation of qi*
heart : fire *warming*
spleen : earth *transformation*
lungs : metal *clearing/cleansing*
kidneys : water *regulation of metabolism*

A TIP FROM THE MASTER

In Traditional Chinese Medicine food is categorized according to its nature or energy as cold, cool, warm, hot, or neutral. Eating too many foods with a particular kind of nature can lead to an imbalance in the body that results in illness.

---

nected to one of the five elements. The liver in its role as the regulator of qi is thought to have similar properties to wood. The lungs are felt to having clearing or cleansing properties, which are associated with the clearing or astringent properties of metal. The kidney, which serves as the regulator of metabolism, controller of water, and storehouse of essence is connected with the element of water. The heart is believed to have a warming action and thus is connected to the element of fire. The spleens role in the body is one of transformation and as such it is connected with the earth.

When we eat food, we are linked with the elements of the outside world. For optimal health, meals should be varied and balanced according to the changes of time and season as well as the taste and nature of foods. If we are struck ill it is the result of an imbalance in our bodies. By readjusting the relationship between the organs, through what we eat, we can restore balance and good health.

The Role of Food's Nature and Taste in TCM

In Traditional Chinese Medicine, food can be categorized according to its particular nature and taste. Understanding these properties of food will make maintaining the yin and yang balance in your body an easier concept to master.

In TCM, a food can be catalogued according to its nature or energy as cold, cool, warm, hot, or neutral. Many foods seem to be a natural fit into one of these categories such as scallions having a warm nature. Others are less obvious such as tomatoes being neutral. You can cause an imbalance in your body, which can lead to illness if you eat too much food with a particular kind of nature or energy.

Food also falls into five different categories of taste: sour, bitter, sweet, pungent, and salty. Generally, a food is placed into one of these categories depending upon how the tongue perceives it. As I discussed earlier, the Chinese believe food, depending on its taste, will go to one of the five organs when it leaves the stomach. We must choose foods according to our current state of health. If too much food of any one particular taste is eaten, you risk disrupting the yin and yang balance of your body, which, as you know, can lead to illness.

Modifying a given food's taste value by using spices or complementary foods can reduce the risk of disturbing the yin and yang balance. The ancient Chinese text *Food Cures* advises, for example, that,

A TIP FROM THE MASTER

In Traditional Chinese Medicine food is also categorized according to five different tastes; sour, bitter, sweet, pungent, and salty. It is important to balance your intake by choosing foods from all of the different taste categories. Eating too much of any particular kind of taste is not healthy and will eventually lead to illness. You can modify any given foods taste value by adding spices or balancing it with complimentary foods.

A TIP FROM THE MASTER

In Traditional Chinese Medicine bodies are sorted into six different body types: excessive, deficient, dry, damp, hot, or cold.

"beef goes with rice, lamb goes with millet, chicken goes with wheat, pork goes with millet, fish goes with melons, etc." You can make a meal more balanced by identifying a particular foods taste and nature and choosing other complimentary foods. For example, since beef is considered sweet in taste and cool to neutral in nature and rice is bitter in taste and warm in nature, by combining these two foods you can neutralize the dish to make the meal a moderate one and ultimately easier for your body to digest.

The recipes I have provided later in this book take both the nature and the taste of foods into consideration. Specific foods and spices are chosen to create perfectly balanced meals. In addition in Appendix I, starting on page 298, I have provided a listing of foods commonly used in Chinese cooking along with their properties and therapeutic actions. In Appendix IV, *The Nature of Common Foods*, starting on page 370 I have given you some easy to use charts that will be helpful when designing your own therapeutic meals.

Body Types and Health

The Chinese sort bodies into six different body types: hot or cold bodies, excessive or deficient bodies, and dry or damp bodies. You can achieve and maintain balance by eating foods that are appropriate to your particular body type.

The concept of body type naturally ties in with the idea that foods have a particular nature. For example, if you tend to sweat heavily after eating pungent foods that are hot or warm in nature you probably have a hot body type. People who have this type of body will benefit from eating cold foods like fruits and melons. If, however, you have a cold body type, you should instead choose foods that are hot or warm in nature, such as scallions, chives, garlic, and pepper.

"Traditional Chinese Medicine does recognize individual dietary needs. Proper food selection must take an individual's particular case into account."

It should be noted that Traditional Chinese Medicine does recognize individual dietary needs. Proper food selection must take an individual's particular case into account. Eating for body type is only one factor to consider when deciding what you should or should not eat.

There are a few clues you can look for to help you decide what type of body type you actually have. Following are some basic descriptions of the different body types. Read each one to determine what body type you have.

"Those with cold body types will often find themselves feeling rundown with little energy..."

Hot or Cold Body Types

Those with a hot body type may often find themselves anxious and are easily excited. If you have a hot body type you might also be somewhat aggressive or quick tempered. Hot body types are often very thirsty and usually prefer cold drinks. There is usually a low urine output with hot body types and the urine is normally yellow in color.

Those with cold body types will often find themselves feeling rundown with little energy and with feelings of general poor health. If you have a cold body type you probably seldom feel thirsty and you most often prefer hot drinks. Cold body types tend to suffer from anemia. The urine of a cold body type is often almost clear in color.

Excessive or Deficient Body Types

Excessive body types are usually very hearty individuals who are able to easily fight off viruses and other illnesses. If you are an excessive body type you probably are very strong and it is likely that you do not produce a lot of sweat even when you exert yourself.

Deficient body types, while able to fight off some viruses or illnesses, tend to find illnesses difficult to get rid of when they do come down with something. Those with a deficient body type often tend to feel physically weak, sweat more often than other body types, and physically may appear thin and pale.

"You can correct a coldness of the body by eating warm or hot foods and you can balance out an overheated body by eating cool or cold foods."

Dry or Damp Body Types

Dry body types tend to hold less body fluid. If you have a dry body type your skin is often very dry (sometimes even flaky) and you might suffer from a dry unproductive cough. Dry body types often feel thirsty.

Damp bodies tend to hold on to excessive amounts of body fluid. If you have a damp body type you are more likely to suffer from fluid related illnesses such as hypertension, edema, and diarrhea and you probably experience an uncommonly noisy stomach.

Food Properties and Health

By now you have probably noticed how the nature of foods and body types correspond. You can correct a coldness of the body, for example, by eating warm or hot foods, and you can balance out an overheated body by eating cool or cold foods. If a person with a hot or excessive body type eats too many hot foods, he may suffer from hyperemia,

"My hope is that you will be able to use this information to determine which food choices are best for your body type and specific health situation."

hypertension, or inflammation.

Certainly, it's not easy to recognize a perfect one-to-one relationship between body type and the nature of certain foods. But we can roughly figure out how they relate: hot and warm foods benefit cold, deficient, and damp bodies, while cold and cool foods benefit hot, excessive, and dry bodies. See appendix IV at the back of this book starting on page 370 for some helpful charts on the nature of certain common foods.

Moving Ahead

Now that you have been introduced to some of the basic food-related principles of Traditional Chinese Medicine, you should have a better understanding of how to use food as a tool to improve your health and prevent illness. My hope is that you will be able to use this information to determine which food choices are best for your body type and specific health situation. I, of course, have only provided you with some basic principles here. If you are interested in learning more about these concepts in depth there are many great books available; check your local library or online resources for a variety to choose from.

I want you to get the most benefit from my cookbook that you possibly can. If you were to visit me in my office I could bend your ear with countless stories of how eating this way has completely turned around the lives of so many of my patients. It wouldn't take me long to convince you how life-changing this new style of eating can be. However, since I am unable to sit down with each of you personally, this book is the next-best thing. I have created a simple, easy-to-implement format for you to follow on your journey towards good health.

"If you were to visit me in my office I could bend your ear with countless stories of how eating this way has completely turned around the lives of so many of my patients. It wouldn't take me long to convince you how life-changing this new style of eating can be."

Following are some helpful hints for getting started as well as a selection of my favorite healing recipes. Also be sure to check the appendixes in the back of the book for other valuable healing food information including a listing of common ailments with the foods you should eat and the foods you should avoid with each, as well as helpful meal plans.

I offer you this book with the sincerest hope that it will serve as a guide and you will be well on your way to a healthier and more balanced lifestyle.

CHAPTER 3

How To Use This Book

I have collected my favorite recipes to share with you. With each recipe I have included step-by-step instructions for preparing the dish. As a reminder that food, like medicine, can be used to heal and maintain good health with each recipe I have included details on the therapeutic uses of the dish.

You will notice that throughout the recipes I have used symbols to point out, at-a-glance, the best recipes for curing, preventing, or treating what I have identified as the five biggest health issues plaguing our modern society. I encourage you to flip through and find what recipes work best for your own particular health situation or that of a loved one.

Below I have included a chart of the symbols I have used throughout my recipes:

Hypertension

Heart Disease

Diabetes

Cancer

Weight Loss

A TIP FROM THE MASTER

There are a variety of woks out there to choose from. Talk with the sales representative in your favorite cooking supply store to get some tips for which one is best for you. One of the most common questions I get when people ask me about buying a wok is what size wok they should purchase. Below I have included a chart to help you choose which size wok will work best for you.

What Size Wok is Best for Me?

12" wok : 1 to 3 people

14" wok : 3 to 6 people

16" wok : 7 to 10 people

18" wok : over 10 people

Before You Get Started

Before you get started I would like to share some tips on how to ensure you get the most nutritional benefit out of the dishes you make. Keep in mind that most of my recipes call for the use of a wok. The Chinese like to spend less time cooking meals and more time enjoying them. If you are using a wok many of my recipes can be prepared in 20 minutes or less, leaving you more time to spend with your family and friends. I prefer to use the wok when I cook because it gets hot much quicker than a normal pan and maintains a higher and more even cooking temperature. This allows food to cook faster sealing in more of its nutritional value. However, you certainly can use an iron skillet and achieve similar results.

Proper Food Combinations and Cooking Methods

In Traditional Chinese Medicine, how foods are combined is very important. In fact, the 3000-year-old Chinese book *Neijin* says that "to combine the five tastes properly can strengthen bones and soften tendons; improve the circulation of vital energy (qi) and blood." In other words, a diverse diet is important because single foods cannot provide the range of nutrients a human body needs to remain healthy.

Over our long history, the Chinese have developed cooking methods that tend to bypass many of the unhealthy pitfalls commonly found in Western cooking. Many of the standard cooking and food preparation methods, such as the tips I list below, focus on retaining the inherent nutritional value of the food.

» *Avoid heavy washing of grains and vegetables.*

Rice and wheat flour, which provide starch, protein, Vitamin B, and mineral salt to the diet, are primary sources of food for the Chinese people. You should avoid heavy washing of wheat and rice, because much of their nutritional content—Vitamin B in particular—resides on the grain's surface. The heavy rinsing of rice, for example, can eliminate vital minerals and vitamins.

The nutritional content of most vegetables is concentrated in their skin, which often is high in Vitamin C. I suggest washing vegetables lightly and never soaking them in water, especially after cutting.

It is best to choose fresh organic vegetables whenever possible. Organic vegetables are far less likely to be treated with pesticides and preservatives, and they therefore require less washing to begin with.

A TIP FROM THE MASTER

In Traditional Chinese Medicine qi or chi is the concept of vital force or energy that is thought to be inherent in all things.

"If you wish to salt your food you should wait until the food is almost finished cooking before adding it. Salt shortens cooking times making the foods more difficult to digest as well as causing the meat to be tough."

» Cook vegetables to retain as many nutrients as possible.

The best way to cook vegetables is to sauté them over high heat. Use a little vinegar and starch to help prevent vitamin C loss. The cooking time should be as short as possible to keep the vitamins in the vegetables from being destroyed.

Boiling is not ordinarily as healthy a method of preparing vegetables, however, boiling in moderation is fine. Make sure to cover the pot during boiling, which should help reduce the escape of vitamin B-1 and vitamin C through evaporation.

» Cook meat to make it tender.

Meat and other animal products are usually hard for the body to digest. To make them easier to digest meats should be cooked until tender. If you wish to salt your food you should wait until the food is almost finished cooking before adding it. Salt shortens cooking times making the foods more difficult to digest as well as causing the meat to be tough.

Whenever possible, mix meat with soy sauce or starch before cooking it in a wok. This mixture makes the meat tender and tastier and reduces the amount of vitamins and proteins that are cooked out of the food.

» *Cook foods in the proper dropping order and for the right amount of time.*

When you cook dishes that combine different types of foods, especially vegetables and meats, it's important to begin cooking each food at the right time and for the right *amount* of time. The recipes I share with you here include specific instructions as to the proper cooking times and the proper "dropping order." You should follow the recipes carefully, as they are designed to maximize the healthy properties of each dish.

"Three meals a day, spaced five to six hours apart, will provide the body with all the nutrients it needs and with enough time to digest the food between meals."

Proper Eating Habits

Three meals a day, spaced five to six hours apart, will provide the body with all the nutrients it needs and with enough time to digest the food between meals. Breakfast should provide 30 percent to 35 percent of your daily calories, lunch should provide about 40 percent of your calories, and dinner should provide around 25 percent to 30 percent of your calories.

In the morning, most people need plenty of calories to get going; their appetites, however, are not usually big. Small portions of higher-calorie foods work best for breakfast, which should be

"I trust you will enjoy my recipes as much as I enjoyed writing them down for you. Remember, there is truth in the old adage, 'You are what you eat.'"

eaten at around 7 a.m.

Lunch should replenish the morning's consumption of energy while preparing the body for the afternoon. It should be the highest-calorie meal of the day. Foods relatively high in protein and fat are recommended. It should be eaten around noon.

For dinner eat cooked vegetables and other easily digested foods. As our physical activities diminish in the evening, we need fewer calories. Eating heavier at dinner leads to the storing of nutrients in the body in the form of fat, which can contribute to obesity and its related illnesses. A rich dinner will also give the stomach and intestines more work to do, causing abdominal distension and perhaps disturbing sleep. Traditional Chinese Medicine holds that going to bed with a full stomach may lead to various diseases, due to indigestion and food coagulation. Dinner should be eaten at around 6 p.m.

Now that I have armed you with some basic tips of how food can be used to treat and prevent illness, I hope you feel better prepared to begin your journey toward good health. I trust you will enjoy my recipes as much as I enjoyed writing them down for you. Remember, there is truth in the old adage, "You are what you eat."

PART TWO

CHINESE RECIPES FOR HEALTH

Healing Beverages

Soothingly refreshing and just a bit exotic the healing beverages I have included here for you to try are sure to tantalize your taste buds while they quench your thirst.

Almond Tea

Therapeutic Uses: Hydrates lungs and eliminates congestion. Improves digestion and relaxes the bowels. Helps to prevent cancer, especially lung and intestinal. Removes toxic elements from the body.

Ingredients:

1 tablespoon of sweet almonds

1 teaspoon of green tea

1 cup of water

Directions:

1. Wash sweet almonds with cold water, then smash into pieces.
2. Put green tea into a cup.
3. Put almond pieces into a steel pot and pour in 1 cup of water. Heat over a medium flame and bring to a boil. Pour mixture over the green tea.
4. Cover cup and allow the tea to steep for five minutes before serving.

Serves 2.

A TIP FROM THE MASTER

Sweet almond is considered mild and non-toxic in nature and can be taken with tea regularly. Bitter almond has very little toxicity as well, but should not be used every day.

Chrysanthemum Tea

Therapeutic Uses: Nourishes the liver. Improves vision. Cools the body down internally. Relieves gas and bloating. Lowers blood pressure and facilitates blood circulation.

Directions:

1. Rinse the petals with cold water to remove any dirt. Put petals into a cup.
2. Pour in 1 cup of boiling water. Cover and allow tea to steep for 5–10 minutes before serving.

To make another cup, the previous step can be repeated until water runs clear.

Serves 2.

Ingredients:

1 teaspoon of dried chrysanthemum

1 cup water

A TIP FROM THE MASTER

Chrysanthemum petals, which have a slightly bitter taste, can be grown in your own garden, purchased at many Asian grocery stores, or found online. If you are allergy prone be careful when trying any new foods. You should drink Chrysanthemum tea the same day it is made. It shouldn't be left over night.

Chrysanthemum petals symbolize future joy in China and they are thought to provide energy.

Golden Corn-tassel Tea

Therapeutic Uses: Cools down the body. Acts as a diuretic. Relaxes the liver and enhances gall bladder function. Lowers blood pressure. Lowers blood sugar.

Ingredients:

3 teaspoons of fresh corn tassels

OR

1 1/2 teaspoons of dried corn tassels

1 cup of water

Directions:

1. Rinse tassels with cold water.
2. Drain, cut and put them in a cup.
3. Pour in 1 cup of boiling water and cover the cup. Steep for 10 minutes and serve.

To make another cup, the previous step can be repeated until water runs clear.

Serves 2.

A TIP FROM THE MASTER

Fresh corn tassels work best for this drink. You can collect fresh tassels from the corn and dry them in the sun. Store completely dried tassels in a sealed container.

Heart-healthy Hawthorn Juice

Therapeutic Uses: Refreshes the mind. Improves appetite. Softens blood vessels. Lowers blood pressure.

Directions:

1. Slice the berries and put them into a teapot. Pour in 1 1/2 cups of boiling water.
2. Cover the pot and let mixture sit until cooled.
3. Put sugar into a glass.
4. Pour hawthorn juice mixture into glass and stir well. Serve.

Serves 2.

Ingredients:

7 dried hawthorn berries

1/2 teaspoon of raw sugar

1 1/2 cups water

A TIP FROM THE MASTER

The berries of the Hawthorn tree are a potent antioxidant that have been shown to dilate blood vessels, increase the hearts ability to pump, and improve the supply of energy to the heart. The whole berries can be purchased in many Asian grocery stores as well as online.

Sweet Dragon-eye "Soup"

Therapeutic Uses: Improves appetite. Invigorates the spleen. Relaxes the mind. Enriches the blood.

Ingredients:

10 longan fruits

5 dates

1 teaspoon of brown sugar

4 cups of water

Directions:

1. Remove the shells from the longans.
2. Put longans and dates in a pot. Pour in 4 cups of water.
3. Cover the pot and simmer for 15 minutes.
4. Remove pot from the heat.
5. Add in brown sugar and mix well.

Serves 4.

A TIP FROM THE MASTER

Longans are a tropical berry-like fruit that are growing in popularity in the United States. They can usually be found in Asian grocery stores as well as some natural food stores. The yellow-brown to reddish-brown skin of the fruit when peeled away reveals a whitish, slightly translucent, flesh with the dark seed showing through giving the fruit its unique nickname of Dragon-eye.

Fresh Fruit Nectar

Therapeutic Uses: Hydrates the lungs. Relieves cough, especially effective for flu-related cough. Eliminates congestion. Acts as a diuretic. Reduces fever. Lowers blood pressure.

Directions:

1. Peel the apple and pear; remove their cores and cut into large cubes.
2. Add 4 cups of water into a pot.
3. Add orange peels, sugar, apple, and pear cubes.
4. Cover the pot and simmer for 30 minutes.
5. Allow the mixture to cool before drinking.

Ingredients:

1 apple

1 pear

2 teaspoons of raw sugar

2–3 pieces of fresh orange (or tangerine) peels

4 cups of water

Serves 4.

Golden Fried Wheat Flour Tea 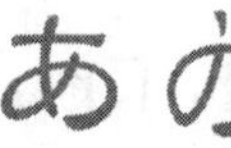 

Therapeutic Uses: Nourishes the spleen to stimulate appetite. Nourishes the skin. Stimulates hair growth. Relieves congestion, constipation and restlessness or insomnia. Relieves cough. Is useful in treating heart disease, hypertension, and cancer.

Ingredients:

1/2 pound of wheat flour

5 teaspoons of olive oil

1/2 cup of almonds

1 teaspoon of salt

Directions:

1. Grind almonds into powder.
2. Combine wheat flour with olive oil.
3. Put the mixture in a pan over low heat and stir-fry until brown.
4. Add in almond powder and salt. Mix well.
5. To serve mix 2 teaspoons of the wheat flour mixture with a glass of water and heat. Serve as you would tea.

Serves 2.

TIP FROM THE MASTER

To make cooking hassle-free, before you even begin to cook, wash and chop your ingredients and arrange them and the cooking utensils in the order in which you will be using them.

Olive Tea

Therapeutic Uses: Promotes the production of body fluids. Reduces fever. Improves the appetite. Channels or balances the flow of qi (energy). Clears the throat and quenches thirst.

Ingredients:

5 or 6 olives

1 teaspoon of raw sugar

5 cups of water

Directions:

1. Put clean olives and 5 cups of water into a pot. Cover and simmer over high heat until the olives begin to break down.
2. Remove the pot from heat. Filter to remove olive pieces.
3. Add sugar into the mixture and mix well.
4. Allow tea to cool before drinking.

Serves 4.

Orange-grove Tea

Therapeutic Uses: Balances the flow of qi. Relieves cough and congestion. Invigorates the stomach. Reduces fever. Enhances skin health.

Ingredients:

1/2 cup of fresh orange or tangerine peels

OR

1 cup of dried orange or tangerine peels

1 teaspoon of raw sugar

Directions:

1. Clean the peels. Tear into small pieces and put into a teapot.
2. Pour boiling water into the pot, cover and allow peels to steep for 5–10 minutes.

Pour into individual teacups and add sugar to taste.

Serves 4.

A TIP FROM THE MASTER

Dried orange and tangerine peels can be purchased in some Asian grocery stores or you can dry your own at home.

Pear Nectar Zing

Therapeutic Uses: Clears the lungs and relieves cough. Eliminates congestion. Cools the body down internally.

Directions:

1. Peel the pears, leaving the stems on, and put them in a pot. Add sugar, orange peels and 4 cups of water.
2. Simmer over medium heat for an hour.
3. Remove and discard pears.
4. Add wine into the mixture and stir well.
5. Allow beverage to cool before drinking.

Serves 4.

Ingredients:

2 pears

1 teaspoon of white wine

1 teaspoon of raw sugar

2 or 3 pieces of fresh or dried orange peel

4 cups of water

A TIP FROM THE MASTER

Use orange peels sparingly. To many may cause your dish to taste perfumed and bitter.

Forest Floor Pine Needle Tea

Therapeutic Uses: Relieves gas and bloating. Removes dampness. Removes obstructions in the channels. Relieves arthritis pain. Helps to prevent the flu and epidemic meningitis.

Ingredients:

1 teaspoon of fresh pine needles

OR

1/2 teaspoon of dried pine needles

3/4 teaspoon of green tea

Directions:

1. Tear pine needles into small pieces and put in a cup with the green tea.
2. Fill cup with boiling water, cover and steep for about 5 minutes. Strain out needles and tea leaves and reserve to make more tea if desired. Serve.

Make more servings by adding boiling water until the water runs clear.

Serves 2.

A TIP FROM THE MASTER

Pine needles collected in the cold winter months when they are new and starchy are the best. Dry them in the sun and store in a sealed container. Pine needles, which are high in vitamin C, produce a mild tasting and refreshing tea.

Perfectly Plum Juice

Therapeutic Uses: Prevents the development of intestinal bacteria and worms. Prevents other diseases of the intestinal tract.

Directions:

1. Put 3 to 4 cups of water and plums into a pot.
2. Cover and simmer over medium heat until the plums turn into pulp.
3. Remove and discard the plums.
4. Add in raw sugar and stir until melted
5. Allow juice to cool and then drink.

Serves 4.

Ingredients:

2 or 3 plums

1 teaspoon of raw sugar

Hot Brown-sugar Toddy

Therapeutic Uses: Warms energy channels. Removes cold from the body. Relieves restlessness and calms the mind. Warms the stomach and eliminates dampness. Relieves menstrual or gynecological problems due to the cold and/or blood congestion.

Ingredients:

1 teaspoon of ginger pieces

5 whole white pepper corns

3 teaspoons of brown sugar

2 cups of water

Directions:

1. Grind white pepper corn.
2. Put brown sugar, ginger and pepper into a steel pot.
3. Add about 2 cups water and simmer over low heat for 3 minutes.
4. Filter and serve while hot.

Serves 3.

A TIP FROM THE MASTER

During menstruation, women should drink a mug of this drink one to two times a day.

Lily and Chinese Red-date Tea

Therapeutic Uses: Nourishes the spleen and stomach. Stimulates the production of fluid. Harmonizes the lung's qi. Enriches the blood. Treats cough.

Ingredients:

3 teaspoons of fresh (or dried) lilies

8 pieces of Chinese red dates

1 tablespoon of raw sugar

Directions:

1. Wash fresh lily and drain. If using dried lily, soak it for 10 minutes before washing.
2. Soak dates in warm water for 5 minutes; wash and drain.
3. Put lily, dates, and sugar together into a soup pot with about 3 cups of water.
4. Simmer over low heat for 1 hour.
5. Remove from heat. Serve.

Serves 2.

A TIP FROM THE MASTER

Check at your local Asian grocery store or online for dried and fresh lilies. Please use caution whenever using edible flowers. Since not all varieties of lily are edible it is better to purchase your lilies from a reliable food supplier instead of trying to pick your own. If you want to grow your own edible lilies check with a local nursery to get advice on what varieties are safe for eating.

Healing Soups

Soups are a staple in the Traditional Chinese Medicine cabinet. Whether you are looking for the thick and hearty yang variety for comfort on a cold day in winter—or the light and flavorful yin variety for a refreshing boost on a summer day—you will find a satisfying soup to fit any occasion and mood in this section.

Bamboo Shoots and Tofu Soup

Therapeutic Uses: Nourishes the blood. Removes heat from the body. Removes toxins from the body. Balances the warm energy of meat. Relieves chronic gastritis. Fights cardiovascular diseases. Good for women who have just given birth.

Ingredients:

1 cup of tofu

2/3 cup of bamboo shoots

1/2 teaspoon of salt

5 cups of chicken stock or water

1/2 teaspoon of pepper

Directions:

1. Cut bamboo and tofu into thin slices.
2. Put 5 cups of water or chicken stock in a wok over high heat and bring to a boil.
3. Slide bamboo and tofu slices into the wok, cook for 5 minutes.
4. Add in salt and pepper to taste.
5. Mix well. Serve.

Serves 2.

A TIP FROM THE MASTER

Tofu is widely available in mainstream grocery stores, natural food stores, and Asian food markets. There are several varieties of tofu available. Experiment to find out the one that you prefer. You may find that you prefer different types for different dishes. For example a softer tofu may work well in a soup, but you may find you prefer the firm variety for stir-frying.

Beef and Spinach Soup

Therapeutic Uses: Nourishes the stomach. Enriches blood and facilitates circulation. Relieves dryness. Relaxes the bowels.

Ingredients:

1/4 pound of beef

1 cup of spinach

5 cups of water, chicken stock, or beef stock

1/2 teaspoon of salt

2 teaspoons of sesame oil

Directions:

1. Slice beef into one-inch squares.
2. Wash spinach and put into boiling water for 30 seconds.
3. Remove and cut into 2-inch strips.
4. Bring 5 cups of water or stock to boil over high heat.
5. Add in beef slices and cook for 5 minutes. Then add spinach strips and cook for 2 more minutes.
6. Add in salt to taste.
7. Mix well. Serve.

Serves 2.

Crucian Carp and White-gourd Soup 

Therapeutic Uses: Facilitates fluid passage to remove swelling. Nourishes the liver. Removes excess heat from the body. Harmonizes the stomach. Helps fight liver disease. Treats abdominal swelling and edema.

Ingredients:

1 pound of crucian (or other suitable) carp

1 pound of white gourd with peel

3 tablespoons of vegetable oil

2 tablespoons of cooking wine

1/2 teaspoon of salt

1/2 tablespoon of green onion pieces

1/2 tablespoon of ginger strips

Directions:

1. Clean fish, removing all internal organs except roe.
2. Wash and drain.
3. Remove seeds from white gourd.
4. Wash and cut gourd into 1-inch cubes.
5. Heat vegetable oil in wok over medium heat. Slide in green onion and ginger, followed by crucian.
6. Cook fish on both sides until golden brown.
7. Add cooking wine and salt.
8. Continue to cook for 1 more minute.
9. Pour in about 5 cups of cold water and bring to a boil.
10. Transfer everything from the wok into a soup pot and add gourd cubes.
11. Simmer over a low heat for 1 hour. Serve.

Serves 4.

A TIP FROM THE MASTER

The white gourd, also know as a wax qourd, can be found in most Asian food markets, many natural food stores, and some mainstream grocery stores as well.

Delicious Dynasty Soup

Therapeutic Uses: Nourishes the stomach and spleen. Excellent for patients during a recovery period. Treats fatigue due to kidney deficiency. Treats hypertension. Reduces high blood sugar.

Directions:

1. Soak the dried shrimp in warm water for 10 minutes.
2. Cut cooked chicken or pork into thin strips.
3. Cut bamboo shoots into slices.
4. Beat and whip eggs in a small bowl.
5. Put about 3 cups of water into a pot and bring to a boil.
6. Add in chicken, shrimp, bamboo shoots, and salt.
7. Bring soup to a boil again. Pour whipped eggs into the pot while stirring quickly.
8. Remove from heat and sprinkle with sesame oil. Serve.

Serves 2.

Ingredients:

10 pieces of dried shrimp

2 eggs

1/4 pound of cooked chicken or pork

1/2 cup of bamboo shoots

1/2 teaspoon of salt

1/2 tablespoon of sesame oil

Tasty Shrimp and Turnip Soup

Therapeutic Uses: Facilitates the circulation of body fluids. Nourishes the kidney. Relieves pains in the knees and loins caused by kidney deficiency. Strengthens bones and muscles.

Ingredients:

3 teaspoons of dried shrimp

1/2 pound of turnips

1/2 teaspoon of salt

1/2 teaspoon of pepper

6 cups of water or chicken stock

Directions:

1. Wash dried shrimp.
2. Wash turnips and cut into 2-inch thin strips.
3. Put dried shrimp into 6 cups boiling water or chicken stock and cook for 5 minutes.
4. Drop in turnip strips and cook for 10 more minutes.
5. Add in salt and pepper and cook one more minute, while stirring to mix well.
6. Transfer the soup to a bowl and sprinkle with sesame oil before serving.

Serves 2.

Fresh Lotus Leaves and Beef Soup

Therapeutic Uses: Invigorates the spleen and stomach. Cleans large intestine. Restores vitality. Treats prolapse of the rectum.

Directions:

1. Wash lotus leaves, pile them together and place in the bottom of a pot.
2. Clean beef and cut into 1-inch cubes.
3. Heat vegetable oil in wok over high heat. Slide in beef cubes and stir-fry for 5 minutes.
4. Add in cooking wine; then cover the wok and allow to simmer for 10 minutes.
5. Transfer beef into the pot with lotus leaves.
6. Add in water to cover about an inch above the beef.
7. Cook over medium heat until boiling.
8. Reduce to low heat and simmer for 1 hour.
9. Add in salt and star anise and continue simmering for another hour, until the beef cubes become very tender. Remove from heat. Serve.

Serves 4.

Ingredients:

4 pieces of fresh lotus leaves

1/2 pound of beef

2 tablespoons of vegetable oil

1/2 teaspoon of salt

2 tablespoons of cooking wine

2 pieces of star anise

A TIP FROM THE MASTER

Please use caution whenever using edible flowers. Since not all varieties of lily are edible it is better to purchase your lilies from a reliable food supplier instead of trying to pick your own. If you want to grow your own edible lilies check with a local nursery to get advice on what varieties are safe for eating. Check at your local Asian grocery store or online for dried and fresh lilies.

Pork Spareribs with Kelp Soup あので

Therapeutic Uses: Nourishes blood and qi. Clears up congestion and other obstructions. Softens blood vessels. Clears heat from the body. Helps to lower blood cholesterol. Prevents fat accumulation. Helps to treat arteriosclerosis, hypertension, diabetes, swollen glands and edema.

A TIP FROM THE MASTER

Kelp is a common sea vegetable often used in Asian cooking. This vegetable is packed with nutrients including calcium, potassium, chromium, magnesium, and iron. Kelp can be purchased in most Asian grocery stores as well as online.

To fully tenderize dried kelp soak it for about one hour in warm water. Alternately, to speed the process, you may simmer the kelp in water for 15 to 20 minutes or pressure-cook it for about five minutes.

Ingredients:

- 1 cup of kelp
- 1 pound of pork spareribs
- 1 tablespoon of vegetable oil
- 3/4 teaspoon of salt
- 3 tablespoons of cooking wine

Directions:

1. Soak kelp in cold water for 2 hours.
2. Rinse kelp and cut into thick strips.
3. Clean ribs and cut into cubes.
4. Heat vegetable oil over medium heat in wok and add ribs. Stir-fry for about 5 minutes.
5. Put in 2 tablespoons of cooking wine and a cup of water. Cover the wok and simmer for about 5 minutes.
6. Remove ribs and place into a soup pot.
7. Pour enough water into the pot to cover about an inch above the ribs.
8. Bring to a boil, then add a spoon of cooking wine.
9. Reduce to low heat and simmer for 2 hours.
10. Add in salt and simmer for another 1/2 hour, allowing the ribs and kelp to become very tender.
11. Remove pot from heat. Serve. Serves 4.

Gingered Lamb Soup

Therapeutic Uses: Replenishes blood to warm the body. Adjusts menstruation to stop cramping and pelvic pain. Treats coldness, stomach pain, and irregular menstruation caused by blood deficiency.

Directions:

1. Rinse Angelica Sinensis and drain.
2. Clean and cut ginger into thick slices.
3. Clean lamb and cut into 1-inch cubes.
4. Heat vegetable oil in wok over high heat. Slide in ginger and stir-fry for 10 seconds.
5. Add lamb cubes and stir-fry for 5 minutes.
6. Add in 2 teaspoons of cooking wine and cover wok, simmering for 5 minutes.
7. Transfer lamb cubes to a soup pot.
8. Add Angelica Sinensis to pot and pour in enough water to cover about an inch above the lamb.
9. Let mixture stand for 1/2 hour.
10. Bring to a boil over high heat.
11. Add in salt, remaining 2 teaspoons of wine and dried tangerine peel.
12. Reduce to low heat and simmer for 1 1/2 hours.
13. Remove from heat. (Discard Angelica Sinensis before eating). Serve.

Serves 4.

Ingredients:

1 tablespoon of Angelica Sinensis (Dong Quai)

2 teaspoons of ginger

1 pound of lamb

3 tablespoons of vegetable oil

1 teaspoon of salt

4 teaspoons of cooking wine

1 dried tangerine peel

A TIP FROM THE MASTER

Angelica Sinensis, also known as Dong Quai, can be purchased online, in most Asian grocery stores, and in many natural food and herbal stores as well.

Kelp Egg Drop Soup

Therapeutic Uses: Nourishes blood and qi. Clears congestion and other obstructions. Helps to lower blood cholesterol and prevent fat accumulation. Specifically treats arteriosclerosis, hypertension, swollen glands, and edema.

Ingredients:

- 1 cup of soaked kelp
- 2 eggs
- 3 teaspoons of green onion pieces
- 1/2 cup of fresh coriander
- 1 tablespoon of sesame oil
- 2 tablespoons of soy sauce
- 7 cups of chicken or pork broth
- 1/2 teaspoon of salt
- 1 tablespoon of cooking wine
- 1 teaspoon of pepper
- 1 cup of cooked white rice

Directions:

1. Cut kelp into 1/2-inch by 2-inch strips.
2. Cut coriander into 1-inch strips.
3. Beat and whip eggs.
4. Heat sesame oil in wok over medium heat; then slide in green onions and stir-fry quickly for 10 seconds.
5. Add in soy sauce.
6. Pour chicken (or pork) broth in and bring to a boil.
7. Add in kelp and salt.
8. Put cooked white rice into wok; add in coriander strips. Bring to a boil and add in whipped eggs. Mix well.
9. Sprinkle on cooking wine and pepper.

Remove from heat. Serve.

Serves 3.

A TIP FROM THE MASTER

Kelp, a nutrition packed sea vegetable, is found in many Asian dishes. Kelp can be purchased in most Asian grocery stores as well as online.

Herbed Lamb Soup

Therapeutic Uses: Nourishes the spleen, kidney, and lungs. Calms the liver. Treats coldness. Enhances the immune system. Helps to treat cancer and chronic fatigue.

Directions:

1. Place lamb spareribs in a large soup pot and add 15 cups (about 4 L) of water.
2. Bring water to a boil. Skim off surface of water.
3. Add in the remaining ingredients.
4. Reduce to low heat and simmer for 4 hours.
5. Remove from heat. Serve.

Serves 8.

Ingredients:

2 pounds of lamb spareribs

1 teaspoon of ginger slices

2 pieces of Angelica Sinensis (Dong Quai)

1 piece of ginseng

3 wolfberry fruits

1 pound of turnip

5 pieces of Chinese red dates

1 teaspoon of salt

A TIP FROM THE MASTER

Wolfberry fruit, resembling a large red raisin when dried, can be found in most Asian grocery stores, many natural food stores, and a number of online sources as well. Angelica Sinensis (Dong Quai) is also readily available in most Asian grocery stores.

Laver, Tofu, and Pork Soup

Therapeutic Uses: Clears away heat and hydrates lungs. Lowers blood pressure and cholesterol. Clears up congestion. Helps to treat hypertension, arteriosclerosis, thyroid-gland enlargement and cough. Helps prevent cancer.

Ingredients:

1 cup of laver (nori)

1/4 pound of pork

1 cup of tofu

1/2 teaspoon of salt

1 tablespoon of cooking wine

1/2 tablespoon of starch

1 stalk of green onion

Directions:

1. Tear laver into pieces and put into a large soup bowl.
2. Chop green onion into small pieces and set aside.
3. Wash pork and cut into thin slices and place into a soup bowl; add salt, cooking wine, and starch. Mix well.
4. Cut tofu into thick pieces.
5. Put 5 cups of water in a wok over medium heat and bring to a boil. Slide tofu into boiling water and add remaining salt.
6. Bring to a boil over medium heat.
7. Put pork slices into the wok and cook for another 5 minutes.
8. Sprinkle green onion pieces and remove wok immediately from the heat.
9. Pour soup into the bowl with laver. Add soy sauce to taste. Serve. Serves 2.

A TIP FROM THE MASTER

Laver is a sea vegetable also known as nori. It can be found in most Asian grocery stores as well as through some online resources.

Sweet Red Bean Soup

Therapeutic Uses: Reduces heat from the body. Removes toxins from the body. Enriches the blood. Calms the mind. Lifts qi. Lowers blood pressure. Acts as a diuretic. Relieves swelling.

Ingredients:

1/2 pound of red beans (kidney beans)

10 dates

3 teaspoons of brown sugar

7 cups of water

Directions:

1. Put the cleaned red beans into a pot.
2. Add 7 cups of water.
3. Cover the pot and simmer for 40 minutes.
4. When red beans have opened up, add dates.
5. Cover and simmer for another 15–20 minutes.
6. Remove the pot from heat, mix in brown sugar, and serve.

Serves 4.

A TIP FROM THE MASTER

For variety this soup can be served over plain white rice or brown rice.

Mung Bean Soup

Therapeutic Uses: Cleans the gall bladder. Nourishes the stomach. Moistens the throat. Clears away body heat. Quenches thirst. Helps to treat chronic cholecystitis.

Ingredients:

1/2 pound of mung beans

2 tablespoons of raw sugar

5 cups cold water

Directions:

1. Wash mung beans and put into a soup pot; then pour in 5 cups of cold water.
2. Simmer over medium heat for half an hour.
3. Add in raw sugar.
4. Reduce to low heat and simmer for another half-hour, until the beans soften.
5. Remove pot from heat. Serve.

Serves 4.

A TIP FROM THE MASTER

Mung beans, which have a yellow to green flesh and a slightly sweet flavor, are found in many Chinese and Indian dishes. You can purchase mung beans in most Asian and Indian food markets and many mainstream grocery stores.

Mushroom and Snow Peas Soup あので

Therapeutic Uses: Nourishes the skin. Replenishes protein in the body. Lowers cholesterol. Helps to treat hypertension and diabetes.

Directions:

1. Soak dried mushrooms in 7 cups of warm water for 15 minutes. Remove the mushrooms. Filter water to remove sediment and dirt.
2. Put mushrooms and water into a pot. Add in snow peas, olive oil, salt, soy sauce, starch, and ginger.
3. Cover the pot and cook over medium heat for 10 minutes.
4. Transfer mixture to a bowl. Serve.

Serves 3.

Ingredients:

1 cup of dried mushrooms

1 cup of snow peas

1 tablespoon of olive oil

1/2 teaspoon of salt

1 teaspoon of soy sauce

1 tablespoon of starch

1/2 tablespoon of ginger slices

7 cups warm water

Pork and Green-bean-sprouts Soup 

Therapeutic Uses: Clears away heat from the body. Quenches thirst. Stimulates milk production for new mothers. Helps to reduce high postpartum blood pressure.

Ingredients:

1/2 pound of pork

1 cup of green bean sprouts

2 stalks of green onion

1/2 tablespoon of starch

1 tablespoon of olive oil

1 tablespoon of cooking wine

1/2 teaspoon of salt

7 cups of water of broth

Directions:

1. Wash and slice pork into thin strips.
2. Combine with salt, cooking wine and starch. Mix well.
3. Wash and drain green bean sprouts. Let stand.
4. Heat olive oil in wok over high heat.
5. Add in sprouts and stir-fry for 1 minute.
6. Pour in about 7 cups of water or broth. Bring to a boil and add pork strips.
7. Simmer for 5 minutes.
8. Sprinkle with green onion pieces. Serve

Serves 4.

Ribs, Peanuts, and Lotus Root Soup

Therapeutic Uses: Nourishes the stomach and blood. Invigorates the stomach and spleen. Improves joint flexibility. Stimulates milk production. Helps to treat chronic stomach diseases such as gastritis, gastroduodenal ulcer, and ptosis of the stomach. Combats anemia and intestinal bleeding. Fights osteoporosis.

Ingredients:

1 pound of pork ribs

1/2 cup of lotus root

2 tablespoons of peanuts

3 teaspoons of ginger

2 stalks of green onion

1 teaspoon of salt

Directions:

1. Chop the ribs into small pieces.
2. Cut lotus root into 1-inch thick pieces.
3. Cut the ginger into big slices.
4. Cut each green onion stalk into 4 parts.
5. Pour cold water into a soup pot to fill it up to 3/4 full.
6. Add ribs to water and bring to a boil. Skim water surface.
7. Reduce to low heat and add peanuts, lotus-root chunks, ginger, onions and salt.
8. Simmer for about 40 minutes over low heat, until food is tender.

Remove pot from heat. Serve.

Serves 6.

A TIP FROM THE MASTER

Lotus root, the edible root of the water lotus plant, can be purchased both fresh and dried in most Asian grocery stores as well as through online sources. Whenever possible use the fresh root instead of the dried variety.

Sweet and Sour Cold Tomatoes あの

Therapeutic Uses: Helps create body fluid. Increases appetite. Harmonizes the function of blood vessels and reduces blood pressure. Clears away heat and toxic materials from the body. Helps to stop capillary bleeding. Helps to treat cardiovascular disease in the summer.

Ingredients:

2 tomatoes

1 tablespoon of honey

Directions:

1. Wash tomatoes with cold water. Cut into thick pieces and place into a bowl.
2. Add honey to the bowl and coat tomato pieces evenly.
3. Cover the bowl and let stand for 1 to 2 hours, until most of the tomato juice has come out of the fruit. Serve.

Serves 2.

Sour Noodle Soup

Therapeutic Uses: Stimulates the production of body fluid. Nourishes the stomach and spleen. Dissipates heat inside the body. Helps treat the flu, cardiovascular diseases, and obesity.

Directions:

1. Cut tofu into half-inch cubes and cabbage into 1-inch strips.
2. Cook noodles in boiling water according to package directions.
3. Add tofu cubes and cabbage strips to noodles and bring to a boil.
4. Remove food from water and separate into four individual serving bowls.
5. Heat chicken broth in a soup pot and add salt, vinegar and soy sauce. Bring to a boil.
6. Pour chicken broth to fill each of the serving bowls. Serve.

Serves 4.

Ingredients:

1/2 pound of Chinese noodles

1/3 pound of Chinese cabbage

2 tablespoons of vinegar

1 tablespoon of soy sauce

1/2 pound of tofu

1 teaspoon of salt

1 1/2 tablespoon of green onion pieces

10 cups of chicken broth

A TIP FROM THE MASTER

Chinese noodles can be purchased in most mainstream grocery stores, natural food stores, Asian food markets, and online.

Soybean and Pork Spareribs Soup 

Therapeutic Uses: Helps to enrich blood and nourishes the liver. Strengthens bones and kidneys. Replenishes qi. Reduces swelling and edema. Helps to treat hypertension, diabetes, edema, and anemia.

Ingredients:

1 pound of soybeans

2 pounds of pork spareribs

1 teaspoon of salt

2 tablespoons of vegetable oil

2 tablespoons of cooking wine

2 stalks of green onion

Directions:

1. Soak soybeans in water for 1 hour, drain, and let stand.
2. Cut green onion into 1-inch pieces, using only the white of the onion.
3. Wash spareribs and cut into 2-inch pieces.
4. Heat vegetable oil in a wok over high heat.
5. Slide in green onions and stir-fry for 5 minutes.
6. Add 1 tablespoon of cooking wine, salt, and spareribs.
7. Cover the wok and simmer for 8 minutes.
8. Transfer ribs and soybeans into a soup pot.
9. Pour just enough water into the pot so that the solids are immersed.
10. Cook over high heat until the water boils.
11. Add remaining cooking wine; then reduce to low heat and simmer for almost 3 hours.
12. Remove pot from heat when soybeans and ribs are soft. Serve.

Serves 6.

A TIP FROM THE MASTER

Whole soybeans are very similar in size and color to green peas. Fresh and dried soybeans can be found in Asian food markets as well as online. If you are unable to find fresh soybeans frozen soybeans are available in most food stores.

Spinach and Pork Soup

Therapeutic Uses: Nourishes the stomach. Promotes blood circulation. Used to treat hypertension. Purges pathogenic heat and enriches the blood. Relieves dryness. Relaxes the bowels. Helps fight cancer.

Directions:

1. Remove any yellow leaves and root hairs from fresh spinach; then wash, drain, and set aside.
2. Slice pork into thin strips and put into a bowl.
3. Add in 1/2 teaspoon of salt, 1 tablespoon cooking wine and 1/2 tablespoon of starch to pork. Mix well.
4. Put 8 cups of water (even better if chicken or pork broth is used) in a wok over medium heat to boil.
5. Put in remaining salt and 1/2 tablespoon of olive oil; then slide in pork strips and cook for 3 minutes.
6. Add spinach and cook for another 3 minutes.
7. Remove from heat and serve.

Serves 4.

Ingredients:

1/2 pound of spinach

1/2 pound of pork

1 teaspoon of salt

1 tablespoon of cooking wine

1/2 tablespoon of starch

1/2 tablespoon of olive oil

8 cups of water, chicken broth or pork broth

Simple and Sweet Sticky-rice Soup

Therapeutic Uses: Warms the body internally. Enriches blood and adjusts qi. Nourishes skin. Helps to regulate abnormal menstruation.

Ingredients:

1 cup of sticky (glutonous) rice

1/2 cup of lotus seeds

10 pieces of red date

2 tablespoons of brown sugar

Directions:

1. Place all ingredients in a pot with 8 cups of water.
2. Bring to a boil over high heat.
3. Reduce to low heat and simmer for 1 hour, until the lotus seeds and sticky rice appear to have melted. Serve.

Serves 3.

A TIP FROM THE MASTER

Lotus seeds, which have a delicately sweet and nutty flavor, can be purchased in most Asian grocery stores as well as from a number of online sources.

Tomato and Pork Soup

Therapeutic Uses: Stimulates the production of body fluid. Removes obstructions in blood vessels. Nourishes the liver and spleen. Facilitates digestion. Helps prevent hypertension. Helps treat chronic liver or gall bladder diseases. Helps treat cancer.

Directions:

1. Wash and cut tomatoes into thick slices.
2. Chop green onion into small pieces.
3. Cut pork into thin slices and mix well with salt, vegetable oil, cooking wine and starch.
4. Heat vegetable oil in a wok over high heat. Slide tomato slices into wok and stir-fry for 2 minutes.
5. Pour 6 cups of water into wok and bring to a boil.
6. Add pork and continue boiling for another 5 minutes.
7. Sprinkle in green onion pieces before serving.

Serves 2.

Ingredients:

3 tomatoes

1/3 pound of pork

1 tablespoon of vegetable oil

1 teaspoon of salt

1 tablespoon of cooking wine

1/2 tablespoon of starch

1 stalk of green onion

6 cups of water

Hearty Pork, Tofu, and Towel Gourd Soup

あので

Therapeutic Uses: Clears away heat and cools the blood. Removes congestion. Facilitates the circulation of body fluid. Helps treat cardiovascular disease, chronic respiratory-system disease, diabetes and milk deficiency in women.

Ingredients:

- 2 towel gourds
- 1/4 pound of pork
- 1/3 pound of tofu
- 1 teaspoon of salt
- 1/2 tablespoon of starch
- 1 stalk of green onion
- 1 tablespoon of cooking wine
- 5 cups of water

Directions:

1. Scrape off gourd peel, wash and cut into cubes.
2. Cut green onion into small pieces.
3. Wash pork, cut into thin slices and put into a bowl.
4. Add 1/2 teaspoon of salt, 1 tablespoon of cooking wine, and 1/2 tablespoon of starch to the pork. Mix well.
5. Cut tofu into half-inch cubes.
6. Pour 5 cups of water into a wok and bring to a boil over medium heat.
7. Slide in pork slices, tofu cubes, and remaining salt.
8. Cook until the mixture boils again; then add in towel gourd and continue cooking for another 3 minutes. (Do not let the gourd turn yellow).
9. Sprinkle green onions on top and serve.

Serves 2.

A TIP FROM THE MASTER

Towel gourds can be found in most Asian markets. This gourd is very fibrous and in the past people would separate the flesh from the seeds and rind and use it as a sponge or towel thus giving it its unique name.

Savory Spiced Turnip and Lamb Soup 

Therapeutic Uses: Nourishes spleen and stomach. Warms lungs and clears up congestion. Restores vitality and fights coldness. Helps treat tuberculosis. Helps treat obesity.

Ingredients:

1/2 pound of lamb

1/2 pound of turnips

1/3 pound of carrots

2 pieces of dried orange peels

3 pieces of ginger slices

3 tablespoons of vegetable oil

1 teaspoon of salt

2 tablespoons of cooking wine

Directions:

1. Wash lamb and cut into 2-inch pieces, drain and let stand.
2. Clean turnips and carrots; then cut into 1-inch pieces.
3. Heat vegetable oil in a wok over high heat.
4. Add in ginger slices and stir-fry several minutes.
5. Slide in lamb pieces and stir-fry for 5 minutes.
6. Pour cooking wine into the wok and stir-fry for another 3 minutes.
7. Pour a half a cup of cold water into the wok and simmer for 10 minutes.
8. Remove the lamb and put together with dried orange peels into a big soup pot.
9. Add just enough cold water so that the lamb is immersed.
10. Bring to a boil over medium heat and then add remaining cooking wine and salt.
11. Reduce to low heat and simmer for half an hour.
12. Add turnip and carrots to the pot and simmer for another hour.
13. When lamb and turnips turn soft, remove the pot from the heat. Serve.

Serves 4.

Snappy Water Chestnut with Lotus Root Soup

Therapeutic Uses: Clears away heat and toxins. Stops bleeding. Quenches thirst. Removes blood from urine. Helps treat obesity.

Ingredients:

7 cups of water or broth

1/2 cup of fresh water chestnuts

1/2 cup of fresh lotus root

7 cups of water or broth

Directions:

1. Remove hair from water chestnut's peel. Wash and drain.
2. Cut chestnuts into halves.
3. Wash lotus roots and cut each in two.
4. Put water chestnuts and lotus roots into a big soup pot.
5. Pour in 7 cups of water or broth.
6. Simmer over low heat for half an hour. Remove from heat. Serve.

Serves 2.

A TIP FROM THE MASTER

Fresh water chestnuts and lotus roots can be found in most Asian grocery stores.

Chinese Cabbage and Tofu Soup

あので

Therapeutic Uses: Nourishes the stomach and intestines. Clears away heat from the body. Dissolves blood coagulation. Helps lower blood pressure and cholesterol. Helps treat diabetes.

Directions:

1. Pull yellow leaves and roots off the cabbage.
2. Wash, drain and cut cabbage diagonally into two parts.
3. Cut tofu into thick pieces.
4. Pour 7 cups of water into a wok over medium heat.
5. Bring water to a boil and slide in tofu. Salt to taste.
6. Bring to a boil again and add in the cabbage.
7. Cook for another 5 minutes and then remove wok from heat.
8. Sprinkle a little sesame oil into the soup before serving.

Serves 2.

Ingredients:

1/3 pound of Chinese cabbage

1 cup of tofu

1/2 teaspoon of salt

1/2 tablespoon of sesame oil

7 cups of water

A TIP FROM THE MASTER

There are two basic types of Chinese cabbage or Pe-tsai: the Chihli type of cabbage is longer and cylindrical in shape and the Napa, or Won Bok, variety is shorter with more bluntly shaped leaves. Either variety can be used in these recipes and both kinds can be purchased in Asian grocery stores, natural food stores, and many mainstream grocery stores.

Young Chinese Cabbage With Pig Soup

Therapeutic Uses: Invigorates the liver and the gall bladder. Clears intestines. Nourishes the stomach. Fights cancer. Helps to treat liver diseases.

Ingredients:

1/2 pound of young Chinese cabbage

1/3 pound of pig liver

1 tablespoon of olive oil

1 teaspoon of salt

2 tablespoons of cooking wine

1 tablespoon of cornstarch

7 cups of water

Directions:

1. Clean cabbage. Soak in water for 5 minutes and rinse.

3. Clean and rinse liver.

4. Cut liver into thin slices and combine with salt, cooking wine and cornstarch. Mix well.

5. Pour 7 cups of water into a wok over high heat.

6. Bring to a boil and slide in cabbage, olive oil and salt.

7. When it boils again, add in liver slices and cook for 2 minutes. Remove from heat. Serve.

Serves 3.

A TIP FROM THE MASTER

Since pig liver is high in cholesterol, people with hypertension or cardiovascular disease should avoid this dish. Chinese cabbage can be purchased in an Asian food market, a natural food store, or in some mainstream grocery stores.

Healing Meat Dishes

Anything but boring,
the wide variety of
meat dishes I have gathered
for you here range from
traditionally simple and rustic
to unusually elegant and exotic.

Beef With Bamboo Shoots

Therapeutic Uses: Nourishes blood. Clears heat inside the body. Helps detoxify the body. Nourishes the spleen and the stomach. Replenishes blood. Strengthens bones and muscles.

Ingredients:

1/3 pound of beef

1/3 pound of bamboo shoots

2 stalks of green onion

1/2 tablespoon of ginger chips

1/3 tablespoon of raw sugar

1/2 teaspoon of pepper

1 tablespoon of soy sauce

2 tablespoons of cooking wine

1 tablespoon of sesame oil

1/2 teaspoon of salt

4 tablespoons of vegetable oil

1 tablespoon of starch

1 1/2 cups of water

Directions:

1. Cut beef into strips.
2. Combine beef with 1/2 tablespoon of starch and cooking wine. Mix well.
3. Cut green onions (using only the white sections) and bamboo shoots into strips.
4. Melt remaining starch in 1/2 cup of water.
5. Heat 2 tablespoons of vegetable oil in wok over high heat.
6. Slide in beef strips and stir-fry for 1 minute. Remove from wok and let stand.
7. Heat remaining oil and slide in bamboo shoot, green onion and ginger; stir-fry for 20 seconds.
8. Pour soy sauce, cooking wine, sugar, 1 cup of water, and remaining melted starch into wok.
9. Slide in beef strips and stir-fry 1 minute; then add in pepper, sesame oil, and salt. Mix well. Serve.

Serves 2.

A TIP FROM THE MASTER

Bamboo shoots have a cooling effect and are often used in meat dishes to balance out the warm energy of the meat.

Beef With Chestnuts

Therapeutic Uses: Nourishes the spleen and kidney. Strengthens muscles and bones. Replenishes qi and blood. Helps to treat softness in the waist and knee, as well as frequent urination due to kidney deficiency. Treats the effects of a weak spleen and stomach.

Directions:

1. Wash beef and boil for 30 minutes.
2. Remove beef and cut into 3-inch by 1-inch pieces.
3. Cut ginger into thin slices and green onion into 2-inch strips.
4. Cut a notch on each chestnut; then put them into boiling water for 10 minutes to soften and remove shells.
5. Heat vegetable oil in wok over high heat. Put in chestnuts and beef separately to stir-fry until browned.
6. Remove and drain oil in the wok. Let chestnuts and beef stand separately.
7. Put green onion strips and ginger slices into wok and stir-fry for 10 seconds; then put the beef back in along with salt, pepper, cooking wine and 1 1/2 cups of water.
8. Bring to a boil and skim off residual layer on the surface. Reduce heat and simmer 20 minutes.
9. Add chestnuts and simmer for another 15 minutes. Serve.

Serves 4.

Ingredients:

1 pound of beef

1 cup of chestnuts

1 teaspoon of ginger pieces

1 stalk of green onion

2 tablespoons of soy sauce

1/4 tablespoon of pepper

1/2 teaspoon of salt

2 tablespoons of cooking wine

2 tablespoons of vegetable oil

A TIP FROM THE MASTER

Meats supply us with needed protein and provide a yang aspect to our food. Although meat is always considered yang in nature the more fatty a meat is the more yin qualities it contains.

Ginger Beef

Therapeutic Uses: Nourishes the spleen and the stomach. Replenishes blood. Strengthens bones and muscles.

Ingredients:

1 pound of beef

1/5 cup of ginger pieces

3 tablespoons of vegetable oil

1 teaspoon of salt

1 tablespoon of cooking wine

Directions:

1. Shave ginger and cut into pieces.
2. Cut beef into 1-inch square slices.
3. Make sauce by mixing cooking wine and salt.
4. Heat 2 tablespoons of vegetable oil in wok over high heat.
5. Slide in beef slices and stir-fry for 3 minutes.
6. Remove and drain oil from beef.
7. Heat remaining oil, slide in ginger pieces, and stir-fry for 1 minute; then pour in the sauce.
8. When the sauce boils, slide in beef slices and stir-fry for another 2 minutes. Serve.

Serves 4.

A TIP FROM THE MASTER

Ginger can be irritating if you have a cough or are congested.

Seared Beef With Turnip あので

Therapeutic Uses: Nourishes spleen and stomach. Strengthens muscles and bones. Stimulates blood circulation. Helps to treat hypertension and diabetes.

Directions:

1. Wash and peel turnips; then slice them into thin strips.
2. Wash beef, slice, and cut into thin strips.
3. Combine beef with 1/4 teaspoon of salt, 1 tablespoon of cooking wine, 1/2 tablespoon each of soy sauce and starch. Mix evenly and let stand.
4. Heat 1 tablespoon of vegetable oil over high heat; then slide turnip strips into wok and stir-fry for 1 minute.
5. Add remaining salt. Remove from wok and let stand.
6. Heat remaining 3 tablespoons of vegetable oil over high heat; then slide in beef strips and cook for 3 minutes.
7. Slide in turnip strips and stir; then add remaining tablespoon of cooking wine and 4 tablespoons of water.
8. Simmer for 5 minutes; then sprinkle in green onion pieces and mix well. Serve.

Serves 3.

Ingredients:

1 pound of turnip

1/2 pound of lean beef

4 tablespoons of vegetable oil

2 tablespoons of cooking wine

4 tablespoons of water

1/2 teaspoon of salt

1/2 tablespoon of soy sauce

1/2 tablespoon of starch

1 stalk of green onion

Bitter Melon with Minced Pork あので

Therapeutic Uses: Clears away heat inside the body. Removes toxins. Lowers blood sugar. Serves as an ideal food for treating diabetes, hypertension, and high cholesterol.

Ingredients:

1 pound of bitter melon

1/3 pound of minced pork

1 tablespoon of soy sauce

1 tablespoon of cooking wine

1 teaspoon of salt

1/2 tablespoon of raw sugar

2 tablespoons of vegetable oil

1/2 tablespoon of green onion bits

1/2 tablespoon of ginger bits

Directions:

1. Wash bitter melon, cut it in half vertically, and remove the seeds; then cut the melon into thick slices.
2. Heat vegetable oil in wok over high heat; then slide in minced pork and stir-fry for 3 minutes.
3. Add in ginger, green onion, soy sauce, and cooking wine and stir-fry for 30 seconds.
4. Slide in bitter melon and stir-fry for 3 minutes.
5. Add in salt and sugar. Mix well. Serve.

Serves 3.

A TIP FROM THE MASTER

Bitter melon is actually a member of the gourd family. It is a close relative of squash, watermelon, and cucumber. The melon resembles a cucumber in general size and color and has a very bumpy surface.

Bitter melon can be purchased in most Asian and natural food stores.

Egg with Pork Strips

Therapeutic Uses: Treats fatigue. Reverses poor appetite due to overworking of the spleen. Helps patients to regain strength and reduces thirst during convalescence. Treats dry cough. Nourishes the blood.

Directions:

1. Slice pork into thin 2-inch strips.
2. Combine salt, starch, and 1/2 cup of water. Mix well and set aside.
3. Beat and whip eggs; pour over pork strips and mix evenly.
4. Heat vegetable oil over high heat, add all other ingredients and stir-fry for 5 minutes. Serve.

Serves 2.

Ingredients:

1/2 pound of lean pork

2 eggs

1/2 teaspoon of salt

1 tablespoon of starch

2 tablespoons of vegetable oil

1/2 cup of water

A TIP FROM THE MASTER

Since egg yolk is high in cholesterol, those with heart disease should avoid this dish.

Fresh Snow Peas With Pork

Therapeutic Uses: Provides energy. Nourishes the spleen and stomach. Clears away excess heat from the body. Helps treat hypertension and diabetes.

Ingredients:

1/3 pound of fresh snow peas

1/3 pound of lean pork

2 tablespoons of cooking wine

1 teaspoon of salt

1/2 tablespoon of starch

2 tablespoons of vegetable oil

1 1/2 cup water

Directions:

1. Cut lean pork into short, thin slices.
2. Combine with half of the salt, 2 tablespoons of cooking wine, 1/2 cup of water and starch. Mix well and let stand.
3. Boil snow peas in water for 6 minutes. Drain and let stand.
4. Heat vegetable oil in wok over high heat. Put in pork slices and stir-fry for 3 minutes.
5. Add 1 cup of water, then add the snow peas and remaining salt and cook for another 5 minutes.
6. Remove from heat. Serve.

Serves 3.

Tender Lamb Strips With Onion

Therapeutic Uses: Replenishes blood to warm the body. Stops painful menstruation. Used to treat coldness, stomach pain, and irregular menstruation due to blood deficiency.

Directions:

1. Wash and cut lamb and onion into strips.
2. Melt starch in 1/2 cup of water.
3. Heat vegetable oil in wok over high heat. Slide in lamb strips and stir-fry for 1 minute.
4. Slide in onion strips and stir-fry for 3 minutes.
5. Add in cooking wine, soy sauce, sugar and remaining 1/2 cup of water. Continue stir-frying for 2 minutes.
6. Pour in melted starch. Stir for 30 seconds to mix well with onions and lamb.
7. Remove from heat. Serve.

Serves 2.

Ingredients:

- 1/2 pound of lamb
- 2/3 of a medium onion
- 2 tablespoons of soy sauce
- 1 tablespoon of raw sugar
- 1/2 teaspoon of salt
- 2 teaspoons of starch
- 3 tablespoons of vegetable oil
- 2 tablespoons of cooking wine
- 1 cup of water

A TIP FROM THE MASTER

Onions can create intestinal gas in people who are sensitive.

Savory Lamb with Sweet and Tangy Carrots

あの

Therapeutic Uses: Warms stomach and restores deficiency. Relieves gas and bloating. Removes cold from the body. Replenishes vital energy. Invigorates yang and enriches the blood. Treats gastric ulcers, hypertension, heart disease, and rheumatic arthritis.

Ingredients:

1 *pound of lamb*

1 *pound of carrots*

1 *tangerine peel*

5 *slices of ginger*

1 *teaspoon of salt*

4 *tablespoons of cooking wine*

1 *tablespoon of soy sauce*

3 *tablespoons of vegetable oil*

7 *cups of water*

Directions:

1. Clean lamb and cut into cubes.
2. Wash carrots and cut into cubes.
3. Dry-fry (without oil) carrots in a wok for 8 minutes; then transfer to a bowl and let stand.
4. Heat vegetable oil over high heat.
5. Slide in ginger slices then lamb and stir-fry for 5 minutes.
6. Add 3 tablespoons of cooking wine and cook for another 7 minutes.
7. Add salt, soy sauce, and 2 tablespoons of cold water and simmer for 10 minutes.
8. Transfer everything into a soup pot; then add the carrots and tangerine peel.
9. Pour in 7 cups of water and simmer over high heat.
10. Add remaining tablespoon of cooking wine, reduce heat and continue simmering for 2 hours, until lamb cubes turn soft. Serve.

Serves 5.

Aromatic Lamb with Crunchy Cucumber

Therapeutic Uses: Replenishes blood to warm the body. Treats painful menstruation. Treats feelings of body coldness, stomach pain, and irregular menstruation due to blood deficiency. Relieves symptoms of hypertension and diabetes.

Directions:

1. Cut lamb into 1-inch square slices and place in a bowl.
2. Combine lamb with starch, 1 teaspoon of soy sauce, and cooking wine. Mix well.
3. Cut cucumber into 1-inch square pieces. Combine with 1/2 the salt and mix well. Set aside.
4. Heat vegetable oil in wok over high heat; then slide in lamb slices and stir-fry for 3 minutes.
5. Slide in green onions, ginger, and cucumber pieces and stir-fry for 3 minutes. Serve.
6. Add in remaining salt and soy sauce and stir several times to mix well.

Serves 3.

Ingredients:

1/2 pound of lamb

1/2 pound of cucumber

2 teaspoons of soy sauce

2 teaspoons of cooking wine

1/2 teaspoon of salt (divided in half)

1 teaspoon of green onion bits

1/2 teaspoon of ginger bits

2 teaspoons of starch

A TIP FROM THE MASTER

The word ginger is derived from the Sanskrit word sinabera meaning "shaped like a horn", because of its antler-like appearance. Although the exact origins of ginger are not known is believed that it was first cultivated in Asia over 3,000 years ago.

Zesty Leek with Bacon in Black-bean Sauce

Therapeutic Uses: Assists in the cure of blood-vessel-related diseases.

Ingredients:

- 1/3 pound of leek
- 1 tablespoon of black-bean sauce
- 1/3 pound of bacon
- 1/2 teaspoon of salt
- 1/2 teaspoon of raw sugar
- 1 tablespoon of vegetable oil

Directions:

1. Wash and cut leek into 1-inch strips.
2. Cut bacon into thin slices.
3. Heat vegetable oil in wok over high heat; then add bacon and black-bean sauce and stir-fry for 3 minutes.
4. Add leek, salt, and sugar to the wok and continue stir-frying for another 5 minutes. Serve.

Serves 2.

A TIP FROM THE MASTER

You can purchase a prepared black bean sauce in an Asian grocery store. You can also make your own by purchasing fermented and salted black beans and adding some rice wine to create a paste.

Lotus Root With Salty Pork

Therapeutic Uses: Nourishes the blood. Treats anemia and bleeding.

Directions:

1. Cut the pork into thin slices and combine with half the salt, a cup of water and starch.
2. Shave the lotus roots and cut into thin slices.
3. Make sauce by mixing soy sauce and remaining salt.
4. Heat vegetable oil over high heat and slide in pork slices and stir-fry for 3 minutes.
5. Put in lotus-root slices to stir-fry for 5 minutes. Pour in the sauce (from step 3) and mix well. Cook 1 minute. Serve.

Serves 3.

Ingredients:

1/2 pound of lean pork

1/2 cup of lotus roots

1 teaspoon of salt

1 tablespoon of soy sauce

1 tablespoon of starch

2 tablespoons of vegetable oil

1 cup of water

A TIP FROM THE MASTER

You can purchase lotus root in most Asian grocery stores, some natural food stores, or online.

Marbled Pork with Chives

Therapeutic Uses: Treats impotence and premature ejaculation. Reduces frequent urination and knee pain caused by a kidney deficiency. Improves digestion.

Ingredients:

- 1/2 pound of marbled pork
- 1/8 pound of chives
- 1 tablespoon of vegetable oil
- 1/2 tablespoon of cooking wine
- 1/2 tablespoon of raw sugar
- 1/2 tablespoon of soy sauce
- 1/2 teaspoon of salt

Directions:

1. Wash pork and cut into thin strips.
2. Wash chives, drain, and cut into 1-inch pieces.
3. Heat 1 tablespoon of vegetable oil in wok over high heat; then slide in pork strips and stir-fry for 1 minute.
4. Add chives and stir-fry 30 more seconds.
5. Pour in cooking wine, soy sauce, sugar and salt. Stir to mix well. Serve.

Serves 3.

A TIP FROM THE MASTER

Meat that is roasted tends to lose much of its energy. Whenever possible meat should be stir-fried to preserve as much of its energy as possible.

Tasty Pork and Eggs

Therapeutic Uses: Treats restlessness and insomnia. Reduces excessive heat in the hands and feet. Stops cough by removing dryness. Invigorates the spleen. Helps new mothers to replenish blood and calcium after giving birth.

Directions:

1. Cut pork into 1-inch strips.
2. Break eggs and whip.
3. Heat 1 tablespoon of vegetable oil in wok over medium heat.
4. Stir-fry eggs for 2 minutes. Remove and let stand.
5. Heat remaining vegetable oil in wok over high heat; then slide in green onion and pork.
6. Stir-fry for 3 minutes; then add in soy sauce, cooking wine, ginger, salt and cooked egg.
7. Add 4 tablespoons of water and continue stir-frying for 5 minutes. Serve.

Serves 3.

Ingredients:

1/2 pound of lean pork

2 eggs

1 teaspoon of green onion pieces

2 tablespoons of vegetable oil

3 pieces of ginger slices

1/2 teaspoon of salt

1/2 tablespoon of cooking wine

4 tablespoons of water

Piquant Pork and Spinach

Therapeutic Uses: Nourishes the stomach. Activates blood circulation. Purges the body of excessive heat. Enriches the blood. Relieves dryness in the body. Relaxes the bowels. Helps prevent cancer.

Ingredients:

1/3 pound of spinach

1/2 pound of pork

2 sprigs of coriander

1 carrot

1 tablespoon of vegetable oil

1/2 tablespoon of soy sauce

1/2 tablespoon of vinegar

1/3 teaspoon of garlic bits

1/2 teaspoon of salt

1/4 tablespoon of pepper

Directions:

1. Wash spinach and quickly boil in hot water for 30 seconds. Remove and drain.
2. Cut into three sections and put them on a plate.
3. Cut carrot into small chunks and boil quickly in hot water for 30 seconds. Remove, drain and place on bed of spinach.
4. Cut coriander into bits and place on spinach.
5. Slice pork into thin strips.
6. Heat vegetable oil in wok over high heat and slide in pork strips.
7. Add pepper and soy sauce and stir-fry for 1 minute or until completely cooked through.
8. Pour pork strips together with sauce over spinach.
9. Add vinegar, salt, and garlic. Mix evenly. Serve.

Serves 3.

A TIP FROM THE MASTER

Garlic should be stored in a well-ventilated, cool, and dry spot away from direct sunlight.

Pan-seared Pork Liver With Turnip

Therapeutic Uses: Fights cancer. Improves vision. Relieves swelling due to a liver deficiency. Clears excessive heat from the body. Improves digestion. Facilitates fluid passage, thus helping to cure hepatitis and chronic cholecystitis.

Ingredients:

- 1/2 pound of pork liver
- 1/2 pound of turnip
- 2 tablespoons of cooking oil
- 1/2 teaspoon of salt
- 1 tablespoon of cooking wine
- 1/3 tablespoon of starch
- 3 teaspoons of green onion pieces

Directions:

1. Clean the pork liver and chop into thin slices.
2. Combine with cooking wine, starch and 1/2 the salt. Mix evenly.
3. Wash turnip and cut into thin slices.
4. Heat 1 tablespoon of cooking oil in wok over high heat; then slide in turnip slices and stir-fry for 4 minutes while adding remaining salt. Remove from wok and let stand.
5. Heat another tablespoon of oil over high heat; then slide in liver slices and stir-fry for 3 minutes.
6. Slide in turnip slices again and continue stir-frying for another 3 minutes.
7. Remove from heat and sprinkle with green onion pieces.

Serves 3.

Fiery Pork Strips with Squash あで

Therapeutic Uses: Clears away excessive heat inside the body. Cools the blood. Facilitates the circulation of body fluids. Treats edema, hypertension, diabetes, and constipation.

Ingredients:

1 pound of squash

1/2 pound of pork

1 hot green pepper

3 tablespoons of vegetable oil

1/2 teaspoon of salt

1 tablespoon of starch

2 cloves of garlic

1/2 cup of water

Directions:

1. Wash and cut pork into 1-inch strips. Combine it with starch and 1/2 cup of water, and mix well.
2. Wash squash and cut into 1-inch squares. Cut hot green pepper into rings. Crush garlic with knife.
3. Heat vegetable oil in wok over high heat. Put in garlic first and then the pork strips to stir-fry for 1 minute.
4. Put in squash pieces and green pepper. Stir-fry for 3 additional minutes. Serve.

Serves 3.

A TIP FROM THE MASTER

If you want to reduce the heat in the chili peppers you are using be sure to remove the seeds and veins from the inside of the peppers before cooking them.

Pork With Celery and Dried Bean Curd 

Therapeutic Uses: Restores deficiency. Improves vision. Facilitates blood circulation while reducing blood pressure.

Ingredients:

3 stalks of celery

1/2 pound of lean pork

1/3 pound of dried bean curd

3 tablespoons of vegetable oil

1/2 teaspoon of salt

1/2 tablespoon of cooking wine

2 tablespoons of water

Directions:

1. Remove celery roots and leaves. Wash and cut stalks into half-inch stems.
2. Wash pork and cut into thin strips.
3. Wash dried bean curd and cut into thin slices.
4. Heat 1 tablespoon of vegetable oil over medium heat; then slide in celery and stir-fry for 2 minutes.
5. Add 1/2 the salt; then transfer to a bowl and let stand.
6. Heat remaining 2 tablespoons of vegetable oil over medium heat; then slide in pork strips and cook for 2 minutes.
7. Slide in bean-curd slices; then add remaining salt and 2 tablespoons of water. Simmer for 3 minutes.
8. Slide in celery and continue stir-frying for 5 minutes. Serve.

Serves 4.

A TIP FROM THE MASTER

Dried bean curd is a dried and pressed version of the more familiar tofu. Made of soybeans, it can be purchased in plastic bags in the refrigerated section of most Asian grocery stores as well as through some online sources

Tofu with Minced Pork

Therapeutic Uses: Relieves dryness. Nourishes yin energy to reinvigorate vital energy. Helps in milk production. Harmonizes the liver and the spleen. Treats chronic liver disease, hypertension, and diabetes.

Ingredients:

1/2 pound of tofu

1/2 pound of minced pork

1/2 teaspoon of salt

2 teaspoons of soy sauce

2 teaspoons of cooking wine

1 teaspoon of raw sugar

1/2 tablespoon of green onion bits

1/2 tablespoon of ginger bits

1/3 tablespoon of garlic bits

1 tablespoon of cornstarch

2 tablespoons of vegetable oil

4 tablespoons of water

Directions:

1. Cut tofu into half-inch cubes, immerse in boiling water for 1 minute, then remove from water and put aside.
2. Heat vegetable oil in wok over high heat; then slide in minced pork and stir-fry for 3 minutes.
3. Add in ginger, green onions and garlic, together with cooking wine, salt and soy sauce. Stir-fry for 30 seconds.
4. Pour in 4 tablespoons of water and then add the sugar.
5. When water boils, slide in tofu cubes and cook for 2 minutes.
6. Sprinkle in cornstarch. Stir quickly for 1 minute until tofu cubes are evenly coated.
7. Transfer to plate. Serve.

Serves 4.

A TIP FROM THE MASTER

Tofu is available in most mainstream grocery stores as well as Asian food markets. This protein packed, naturally bland tasting soybean product readily absorbs the tastes of the foods and sauces you cook it with. Uncooked tofu should be stored in water in a covered container and the water should be changed daily.

Pork Strips with Celery and Carrot

Therapeutic Uses: Rebalances the intestines and stomach. Lubricates the lungs. Treats bronchitis, coughs, hypertension, obesity, and diabetes.

Directions:

1. Wash pork and cut into 1-inch strips.
2. Combine with starch and a 1/2 cup of water. Mix well.
3. Wash celery and carrots; then cut into pieces.
4. Heat vegetable oil in wok over high heat; then slide in carrots and stir-fry for 3 minutes.
5. Slide in celery and pork strips and stir-fry for 3 minutes.
6. Add salt and mix well.
7. Transfer to plate. Serve.

Serves 2.

Ingredients:

3 stalks of celery

1/3 pound of carrots

1/3 pound of lean pork

1 tablespoon of starch

1/2 teaspoon of salt

2 tablespoons of vegetable oil

1/2 cup of water

Pork with Asparagus Lettuce

Therapeutic Uses: Replenishes vital energy. Invigorates the spleen. Facilitates the production of body fluids. Induces milk production. Good for lactating women. Treats diabetes.

Ingredients:

1/2 pound of asparagus lettuce

1/2 pound of lean pork

2 tablespoons of vegetable oil

1/2 teaspoon of salt

1 tablespoon of cooking wine

1/2 tablespoon of starch

1/2 tablespoon of green onion pieces

Directions:

1. Clean and cut asparagus lettuce into strips.
2. Wash and slice pork.
3. Combine with 1/2 of the salt, cooking wine and starch. Mix well.
4. Heat 1 tablespoon of vegetable oil in a wok over high heat; then slide in asparagus lettuce and stir-fry for 3 minutes.
5. Add remaining salt and continue stir-frying for 3 minutes.
6. Transfer asparagus lettuce into a bowl and let stand.
7. Heat remaining vegetable oil over high heat. Slide in green onion followed by pork slices and stir-fry quickly for 3 minutes.
8. Slide in asparagus lettuce and continue stir-frying for 5 minutes.
9. Transfer to plate. Serve.

Serves 3.

A TIP FROM THE MASTER

Asparagus lettuce is a light colored, vitamin-C packed, salad green that is growing in popularity in the United States. The lettuce looks like a cross between celery and lettuce and has a deliciously mild taste resembling a combination of summer squash and artichoke. You can find the lettuce in many Asian grocery stores as well as a number of natural food stores.

Pork with Carrots

Therapeutic Uses: Reinforces and replenishes vital energy. Reduces blood pressure. Improves vision. Serves as a cancer preventive.

Ingredients:

1/3 pound of carrot

1/3 pound of lean pork

3 tablespoons of vegetable oil

1/2 teaspoon of salt

1 tablespoon of cooking wine

1 stalk of green onion

2 tablespoons of water

Directions:

1. Wash carrots and cut into thin slices. Wash onion and cut into pieces.
2. Wash and cut pork into slices; then mix with 1/2 of the salt and 1/2 tablespoon of cooking wine. Let stand.
3. Heat wok over high heat; then slide in carrots and dry-fry (no oil) for 10 minutes. Transfer to a bowl and let stand.
4. Heat vegetable oil over high heat; then slide in pork slices and stir-fry for 3 minutes.
5. Slide in carrots, add remaining salt and remaining cooking wine, and stir-fry for 1 minute.
6. Add 2 tablespoons of water and simmer for 2 minutes. Repeat this step 3 more times.
7. Sprinkle on green onion pieces. Serve.

Serves 2.

A TIP FROM THE MASTER

Whenever possible avoid using frozen meats. The freezing process destroys the meats energy.

Gingered Pork With Chestnuts

Therapeutic Uses: Nourishes the stomach and invigorates the spleen. Nourishes yin energy. Relieves dryness. Treats symptoms of spleen deficiency. Treats cough caused by overheated lungs.

Ingredients:

1/2 pound of chestnuts

pound of lean pork

1/5 cup of ginger slices

3 stalks of green onion

1 tablespoon of soy sauce

2 cups of water

8 tablespoons of vegetable oil

1/2 teaspoon of salt

1/2 tablespoon of raw sugar

Directions:

1. Cut a notch on each chestnut and put them in boiling water for 10 minutes to soften. Remove shells and inner skins.
2. Cut ginger into thin slices and green onions into 1-inch strips.
3. Wash pork and cut into 2-inch cubes.
4. Heat 4 tablespoons of vegetable oil over high heat; then slide in chestnuts and stir-fry for 3 minutes.
5. Remove and drain oil; then transfer chestnuts to a plate and let stand.
6. Remove excess oil, keeping only 2 tablespoons in the wok over medium heat.
7. Slide in ginger, green onion and pork, and stir-fry for 10 minutes.
8. Add 2 cups of water and bring to a boil.
9. Remove residue from the surface of the water. Reduce heat and allow to simmer for 15 minutes.
10. Add chestnuts, salt, sugar and soy sauce and continue simmering for 15 minutes. Serve.

Serves 3.

Pork with Coriander

Therapeutic Uses: Combats fatigue. Treats poor appetite due to overworking of the spleen. Combats weakness and thirst during convalescence. Relieves dry cough due to dryness of the lungs.

Ingredients:

- 1/5 pound of fresh coriander
- 1/2 pound of lean pork
- 1/2 teaspoon of salt
- 1/2 tablespoon of starch
- 2 tablespoons of vegetable oil
- 4 tablespoons of water

Directions:

1. Wash coriander and cut into 1-inch strips.
2. Cut pork into 1-inch thin strips.
3. Combine pork with 1/4 teaspoon of salt, starch and 4 tablespoons of water. Mix well.
4. Heat vegetable oil in wok over high heat; then slide in pork strips and stir-fry for 2 minutes.
5. Add in coriander strips and remaining salt and continue stir-frying for 3 minutes. Serve.

Serves 3.

Sautéed Lamb

Therapeutic Uses: Warms interior energy channels. Replenishes blood. Warms the kidney to restore vitality. Relieves vomiting, weakness, fatigue, and edema. Helps post-labor women combat stomachache, weakness, and loin pain. Treats impotence. Treats cold due to kidney deficiency. Helps treat diabetes.

Ingredients:

- 2 pounds of lamb
- 2 tablespoons of cooking oil
- 1/2 tablespoon of cooking wine
- 2 teaspoons of soy sauce
- 2 tablespoons of fennel
- 2 teaspoons of ginger slices
- 1 teaspoon of garlic pieces
- 1 teaspoon of sugar
- 1 piece of hawthorn fruit
- 5 tablespoons of water

Directions:

1. Wash lamb, first with cold and then with boiling water.
2. Cut lamb into half-inch cubes.
3. Heat oil in wok over high heat; slide in lamb cubes together with wine, ginger slices and fennel strips. Stir-fry for 10 minutes.
4. Add 5 tablespoons of water and the piece of hawthorn. Continue to stir-fry for another 5 minutes.
5. Add in soy sauce and sugar, and continue stir-frying for 20 minutes.
6. Add garlic pieces. Serve.

Serves 5.

A TIP FROM THE MASTER

The reddish-orange apple-like hawthorn fruit has a sweet and tart flavor. The fruit can be found in most Asian grocery stores.

Stewed Leg of Lamb

Therapeutic Uses: Warms up the spleen, stomach and kidney. Strengthens the bladder. Treats those suffering from frequent urination.

Ingredients:

1/2 pound of carrots
2 tablespoons of cooking wine
1 teaspoon of ginger pieces
2 pounds of lamb leg
1 teaspoon of salt
1/2 tablespoon of cassia barks
2 tablespoons of vegetable oil
2 tablespoons of soy sauce
1 cup of cold water

Directions:

1. Clean and cut lamb leg into 1-inch cubes.
2. Wash carrots and cut into 1-inch pieces.
3. Dry-fry (no oil) carrot cubes for 10 minutes; then transfer to a bowl and let stand.
4. Heat vegetable oil in wok over medium heat; then slide in ginger followed by lamb cubes and stir-fry for 5 minutes.
5. Add in cooking wine and stir-fry for another 5 minutes.
6. Add in salt, soy sauce, and 1 cup of cold water. Cover the wok and simmer for 10 minutes.
7. Transfer lamb cubes to a soup pot; then add in carrot cubes and cassia bark.
8. Pour in just enough cold water to immerse the lamb cubes.
9. Bring to a boil over high heat; then reduce heat and allow to stew for 2 hours. Serve.

Serves 5.

A TIP FROM THE MASTER

The cassia tree is an evergreen that was originally a native of China. The bark of the tree is often used as a spice and is an ingredient in many Traditional Chinese Medicine formulations. Like the spice cinnamon, cassia bark has a spicy slightly hot flavor followed by a sweet aftertaste. Dried cassia bark looks much like cinnamon and can be found in most Asian grocery stores. If cassia is unavailable cinnamon may be substituted.

Stewed Lean Pork With Mushrooms

Therapeutic Uses: Relieves abdominal distension or pain due to functional imbalance between liver and spleen. Helps to treat chronic hepatitis and diabetes.

Ingredients:

1/2 pound of lean pork

1/4 pound of mushrooms

1/2 teaspoon of salt

1 stalk of green onion

3 ginger slices

Directions:

1. Cut pork into half-inch cubes.
2. Put pork cubes in a soup pot; then pour in just enough water to immerse them.
3. Bring to a boil over high heat; then add in mushrooms, salt, ginger and green onion.
4. Reduce heat and simmer for 45 minutes to allow pork cubes to become tender. Serve.

Serves 3.

A TIP FROM THE MASTER

You may store unpeeled ginger in the refrigerator in a food storage bag for up to three weeks.

Beef With Snow Peas and Tofu

Therapeutic Uses: Nourishes the spleen and stomach. Harmonizes the stomach. Clears away toxins. Replenishes body in protein. Balances cholesterol level in the body. Helps treat heart disease.

Directions:

1. Cut beef into tiny cubes.
2. Cut tofu into half-inch cubes.
3. Put tofu in boiling water for 20 seconds. Remove and let stand.
4. Heat vegetable oil in wok over high heat; then slide in beef and stir-fry for 1 minute.
5. Add soy sauce, sugar, and 1 1/2 cups of water. Reduce to low heat and simmer for 10 minutes.
6. Add tofu and salt and stir several times; then continue to let simmer for 5 minutes.
7. Add snow peas and starch. Mix well. Simmer for 1 minutes.
8. Sprinkle in garlic and green onion. Mix well and serve.

Serves 2.

Ingredients:

1/3 pound of tofu

1/3 pound of beef

2 tablespoons of vegetable oil

1/3 cup of snow peas

1/2 teaspoon of salt

1/2 tablespoon of starch

1/2 tablespoon of raw sugar

1/2 tablespoon of minced garlic

1 teaspoon of green onion pieces

1/2 tablespoon of soy sauce

1 1/2 cups of water

A TIP FROM THE MASTER

Tofu is now readily available in even mainstream grocery stores. There are several varieties of tofu ranging from soft to firm. Experiment and choose the kind that works best for you.

Gammon, White Gourd, and Mushroom

Therapeutic Uses: Nourishes the spleen and liver. Improves appetite. Improves fluid passage. Nourishes the kidney and facilitates the production of body fluids. Treats liver disease. Helps to prevent cancer.

Ingredients:

1 pound of gammon (specific cut of pork)

1 cup of dried mushroom

1 pound of white gourd

1 tablespoon of cooking wine

1 tablespoon of scallion (the white part)

1/2 teaspoon of salt

Directions:

1. Wash gammon and cut into long slices.
2. Wash and drain dried mushrooms.
3. Wash and cut white gourd into cubes. Put them on a plate (choose one that withstands high heat well), add salt and mix evenly.
4. Put gammon slices on white-gourd cubes and place mushrooms around them.
5. Sprinkle on cooking wine and scallion whites.
6. Put a steamer rack in a steamer pot and fill with water to about an inch under the rack. Bring water to a boil. Lower heat to medium.
7. Carefully place the plate on the rack. Place a cover over the pot, but leave a space for vapor to escape and avoid overflow of water.
8. Steam over medium heat for 45 minutes, or until vegetables are tender.
9. Carefully remove the plate and serve. Serves 5.

A TIP FROM THE MASTER

White gourd, also referred to as wax gourd or Chinese preserving melon, is a common ingredient in many Asian dishes. The gourd is oblong in shape with a white rind that is covered in a fine silky fuzz like that of a peach. White gourds can be purchased in Asian grocery stores and natural food stores.

Healing Poultry Dishes

These deliciously satisfying
poultry dishes are
bound to satisfy
diners with
sophisticated palates
and informal
eaters alike.

Spicy Gingered Chicken

Therapeutic Uses: Provides essential protein and vitamins. Aids in weight loss. Helps treat hypertension and diabetes.

Ingredients:

- 1/2 pound of white chicken meat
- 1 hot green pepper
- 2 tablespoons of cooking wine
- 1/2 teaspoon of salt
- 1/2 teaspoon of pepper
- 2 tablespoons of starch
- 1/2 tablespoon of green onion pieces
- 1/2 tablespoon of thin ginger slices
- 1/2 teaspoon of garlic pieces
- 3 tablespoons of vegetable oil
- 1/2 cup of water

Directions:

1. Cut chicken into half-inch cubes.
2. Combine chicken with 1 tablespoon of cooking wine, water, half of the salt, and 1 tablespoon of starch. Mix well and let stand.
3. Slice hot green pepper into rings.
4. Make sauce by mixing remaining cooking wine, remaining salt, pepper and starch.
5. Heat remaining oil in wok over high heat; then slide in chicken cubes and stir-fry for 3 minutes.
6. Slide in hot green pepper, ginger, green onion and garlic. Stir-fry for another 8 minutes.
7. Sprinkle on sauce and continue stir-frying for 3 minutes. Serve.

Serves 3.

A TIP FROM THE MASTER

Ginger is warm in nature and is a good spice to use in the cold months or to balance out a cool or cold dish.

Chicken With Walnuts

Therapeutic Uses: Invigorates the lungs and kidney. Improves vision. Treats coughing and gasping caused by deficiencies in the lungs and kidney. Reduces dizziness due to anemia. Relieves seniors from chronic inflammation and infection of the trachea.

Directions:

1. Soak walnut kernels in warm water until swelling. Remove skin.
2. Wash wolfberry fruit.
3. Remove and discard egg yolk. Beat egg white.
4. Cut chicken into half-inch cubes.
5. Put chicken cubes in a bowl. Add half of the salt, the beaten egg white and starch. Mix well.
6. Heat olive oil in wok over high heat; then slide in walnut kernels and stir-fry until the mixture turns egg-yellow. Transfer walnuts to a dish and let stand.
7. Slide chicken cubes into wok and stir-fry quickly for 1 minute.
8. Add in green onion, ginger, sugar, and pepper. Stir-fry for 3 minutes.
9. Add in walnut kernels and wolfberry fruit and continue stir-frying for another 3 minutes. Add remaining salt. Mix well.
10. Remove from heat, sprinkle on sesame oil, and serve.

Serves 3.

Ingredients:

- 1/2 pound of white chicken meat
- 2 tablespoons of walnuts
- 1/4 cup of Chinese wolfberry fruits
- 2 eggs
- 1/2 teaspoon of salt
- 2 tablespoons of cooking wine
- 1/2 teaspoon of pepper
- 1/2 teaspoon of ginger pieces
- 1/2 tablespoon of green onion pieces
- 1 tablespoon of sesame oil
- 1 tablespoon of raw sugar
- 2 tablespoons of starch
- 2 tablespoons of olive oil

A TIP FROM THE MASTER

The fruit of the Wolfberry shrub is a bright red berry that is normally harvested in the late summer and dried like raisins or dates. Wolfberry fruit can be purchased in most Asian grocery stores.

Steamed Chicken with Chestnuts

Therapeutic Uses: Nourishes the spleen and stomach. Invigorates the kidney. Relieves chronic gastritis, kidney deficiency, and frequent urination. Treats waist and leg pains experienced by seniors. Strengthens the waist and feet.

Ingredients:

2 pounds of fresh chestnuts

1 chicken (or game hen)

3/4 teaspoon of salt

2 tablespoons of cooking wine

Directions:

1. Cut a notch in the middle of each chestnut and boil for 3 minutes. Drain, remove shells and let stand.
2. Wash the chicken and cut into 1-inch cubes.
3. Mix chestnuts with chicken cubes. Put mixture into a bowl, sprinkle with salt and add cooking wine.
4. Put the bowl into a large steamer and steam for 2 1/2 hours or until meat is very tender. Serve.

Serves 5.

Steamed Duck with Ginger

Therapeutic Uses: Invigorates and nourishes lung energy and spleen. Enriches blood to strengthen the heart. Improves metabolism. Helps to treat the symptoms of bronchitis and tuberculosis.

Directions:

1. Rinse the ginger and place in a small bowl.
2. Place the bowl in a pot with water and steam until soft.
3. Cut ginger into thin slices and let stand.
4. Wash the duck; then place it chest-up in a deep bowl.
5. Insert ginger slices in its belly; then bend the duck head into the belly and sprinkle 1 1/2 tablespoons of cooking wine inside.
6. Sew duck belly up with thread.
7. Add 1 cup of water; then add salt and remaining wine into the bowl. Cover the bowl to keep water vapor out.
8. Fill a steamer with water to about an inch under the steamer rack. Place the bowl on the rack and steam for 3 hours or until duck becomes tender. Serve.

Serves 5.

Ingredients:

1/2 ounce of ginger

1 duck

2 tablespoons of cooking wine

1/2 tablespoon of salt

1 cup of water

A TIP FROM THE MASTER

A metal or bamboo steamer can be purchased in mainstream cooking supply stores, Asian grocery stores, and online.

Stewed Duck Infused with Ginger & Garlic

Therapeutic Uses: Awakens vital energy and facilitates circulation of body fluids. Removes swelling and coagulation. Treats digestive problems (food stagnation). Relieves edema and chronic kidney disorders. Aids in weight loss. Helps to prevent cancer.

Ingredients:

1 duck

3 cloves of garlic

1/5 cup of ginger pieces

2 stalks of green onion

3 tablespoons of cooking wine

1/4 tablespoon of pepper

1/2 tablespoon of salt

10 1/2 cups water

Directions:

1. Completely clean the duck, removing all internal organs and its feet.
2. Cut green onions into 1-inch strips.
3. Peel the garlic and insert into duck's belly.
4. Put 10 1/2 cups of water in a large soup pot.
5. Put duck, ginger, salt, green onion, cooking wine, and pepper into the pot.
6. Bring to a boil over a high heat.
7. Skim residue from the surface.
8. Reduce heat and simmer for 1 hour.
9. Remove from heat and serve.

Serves 5.

Healing Seafood Dishes

Spontaneous get-togethers,
elegant dinner parties,
and leisurely Sunday brunches
are all appropriate events
to serve these versatile
seafood dishes that are
as good for you as they
are good tasting.

Shrimp With Steamed Egg and Garden Fresh Vegetables Soup

Therapeutic Uses: Replenishes proteins in the body. Improves appetite. Treats chronic fatigue resulting from a kidney deficiency. Helps to treat diabetes.

Ingredients:

1/3 cup of soaked, dried shrimp

2 eggs

1/2 cup of snow peas

1/2 cup of mushrooms

2 medium potatoes

1/4 pound of ham

1/2 tablespoon of starch

1/2 tablespoon of sesame oil

1/2 teaspoon of salt

5 cups of water

Directions:

1. Beat eggs evenly in a bowl.
2. Place a steam rack in a pot with water. Place the bowl with the eggs on the rack. Cover 2/3 of the pot, leaving space for vapor to escape and avoid overflow. Bring water to a boil and lower heat to let steam for 15 minutes or until egg is cooked.
3. Remove bowl and cut cooked egg into small pieces.
4. Cut potatoes, mushrooms, and ham into small pieces.
5. Put 5 cups of water in wok over high heat to boil; add dried shrimp, eggs, snow peas, potatoes, mushrooms, ham and salt.
6. When mixture boils again, add the starch.
7. Transfer to a soup bowl.
8. Sprinkle in sesame oil. Serve.

Serves 3.

A TIP FROM THE MASTER

Since shrimp is high in cholesterol those with elevated cholesterol levels may want to avoid shrimp dishes.

Savory Squid with Pork and Chive Strips

Therapeutic Uses: Nourishes the stomach and spleen. Stimulates appetite. Replenishes the body's vital essence. Helps treat lung diseases and constipation. Relieves weariness in the loins and knees due to kidney deficiency.

Ingredients:

1/3 pound of squid (fresh works best)	1/2 pound of pork	1 teaspoon of salt
4 tablespoons of vegetable oil	2 tablespoons of cooking wine	1/5 cup of chives
1/2 tablespoon of raw sugar	1 teaspoon of vinegar	1/2 teaspoon of pepper
2 tablespoons of starch	2 tablespoons of soy sauce	1 egg

Directions:

1. Clean the squid and cut into 1-inch pieces.
2. Cut chives and pork into 1-inch pieces.
3. Remove egg yolk and discard and beat egg white.
4. Put pork in a bowl and combine with the cooking wine, egg white, starch and half of the salt. Mix well.
5. Make sauce by mixing soy sauce, sugar, remaining salt, vinegar, and pepper.
6. Heat 2 tablespoons of vegetable oil in wok over high heat; then slide in pork mixture and stir-fry for 2 minutes.
7. Remove and let stand.
8. Heat another 2 tablespoons of oil, slide in squid and stir-fry for 1 minute.
9. Slide in pork and chives and continue stir-frying for 4 minutes.
10. Pour in sauce and mix well. Serve

Serves 4.

A TIP FROM THE MASTER

Squid, also called calamari, is best fresh and not frozen. You may be able to purchase already cleaned fresh squid from your local fish market or seafood store. If you are going to clean the squid yourself and never have done so before it is best to obtain instructions first. There are a number of online sources to help you with this or you can check at your local library. Cleaning your own is a bit more work, but fresh squid cooked correctly is well worth any extra time you need to spend on it.

Sautéed Eel and Garlic

Therapeutic Uses: Replenishes vital energy in the body. Combats fatigue. Removes dampness and gas in the body. Facilitates blood circulation Reduces blood-sugar levels. Helps to treat rheumatic arthritis.

Ingredients:

- 1 pound fresh eel
- 3 tablespoons of vegetable oil
- 2 tablespoons of cooking wine
- 1 tablespoon of soy sauce
- 1 teaspoon of garlic pieces
- 1/2 tablespoon of green onion pieces
- 1/4 teaspoon of salt

Directions:

1. Remove internal organs from eel, clean and cut into 1-inch strips. Drain and let stand.
2. Heat oil in a wok over high heat; then slide in garlic pieces followed by eel strips and stir-fry for 3 minutes.
3. Add cooking wine. Cover the wok and simmer for 3 minutes.
4. Add in salt, soy sauce and a cup of cold water. Cover and simmer for another 25 minutes, until the eel strips turn soft.
5. Remove and sprinkle with green onions to serve. Eat while hot.

Serves 4.

A TIP FROM THE MASTER

Like any fresh fish, eel will need to be cleaned before you cook it. You may be able to have it cleaned for you in the store where you purchase it, but if not it is a fairly easy process to do yourself. You will need a couple of supplies: a sharp knife, a clean kitchen towel, and a clean pair of pliers. Since eel tends to be slippery grab your kitchen towel and use it to hold the fish on a solid cutting surface. Make a cut around the neck and you will see the thick skin separates. Grab the skin with your clean pair of pliers and pull down the length of the body until you reach the tail and cut the skin free and discard it. Now slice open the stomach and remove the innards. Cut off the head and rinse the cleaned eel under cold water. Now it is ready to slice for cooking.

Shrimp with Cauliflower

Therapeutic Uses: Invigorates the kidney and stomach. Treats weakness in the loins and knees due to kidney deficiency. Helps to prevent cancer.

Directions:

1. Cut cauliflower into small pieces and boil in water for 2 minutes and drain.
2. Soak dried shrimp in boiling water for 10 minutes and drain.
3. Heat vegetable oil in wok over high heat; then slide in cauliflower and stir-fry for 1 minute.
4. Add ginger, green onions and chicken broth; Reduce to low heat, cover the wok, and simmer for 5 minutes.
5. Add salt and sugar.
6. Dissolve cornstarch in a tablespoon of water and pour into the wok.
7. Slide in shrimp, sprinkle sesame oil, and stir. Serve

Serves 3.

Ingredients:

1/2 pound of cauliflower

1/2 cup of dried shrimp

1/2 teaspoon of salt

3 cups of chicken broth

1 tablespoon of cornstarch

1/2 tablespoon of green onion pieces

1 teaspoon of ginger pieces

2 tablespoons of vegetable oil

1 tablespoon of sesame oil

1 teaspoon of raw sugar

A TIP FROM THE MASTER

Since shrimp is high in cholesterol those with elevated cholesterol levels may want to avoid shrimp dishes.

Shrimp in Tomato Sauce

Therapeutic Uses: Stimulates appetite. Facilitates the production of body fluids. Nourishes the kidneys. Helps treat hypertension. Aids in weight loss.

Ingredients:

- 1/2 pound of shrimp
- 1 cucumber
- 1 cup of tomato sauce
- 2 tablespoons of cooking wine
- 1/2 teaspoon of salt
- 2 teaspoons of vinegar
- 2 teaspoons of raw sugar
- 1 tablespoon of green onion pieces
- 1/2 teaspoon of ginger pieces
- 2 tablespoons of vegetable oil
- 2 tablespoons of cornstarch
- 1 egg
- 1 cup of water

Directions:

1. Remove the dark thread on the backs of the shrimp (devein). Rinse and drain shrimp.
2. Combine with half of the salt, 1 1/2 tablespoons of cooking wine, egg white and 1 tablespoon of cornstarch. Mix well.
3. Halve cucumbers vertically and remove seeds. Then cut them into half-inch pieces.
4. Heat 1 tablespoon of vegetable oil in wok over high heat; then slide in shrimp and stir-fry for 3 minutes.
5. Transfer and let stand.
6. Pour remaining oil into the wok; then slide in ginger and green onion pieces and stir-fry for 15 seconds.
7. Add in tomato sauce, remaining cooking wine, remaining salt and a cup of water, followed by vinegar and sugar. Mix well to make sauce.
8. Thicken the sauce by adding remaining cornstarch.
9. Slide shrimp and cucumber pieces into the sauce and stir-fry for 5 minutes, until they are coated evenly with sauce. Serve.

Serves 4.

Salty Shrimp

Therapeutic Uses: Treats pains in the loins and knees. Helps treat obesity.

Directions:

1. Clean and wash shrimp.
2. Cut green onion into 2-inch strips.
3. Put about 8 cups of water in wok over heat; then slide in hot peppers to boil for 5 minutes.
4. Remove and discard the peppers.
5. Slide in green onions, ginger and salt.
6. When water boils, add in shrimp, reduce to medium heat and cook for 8 minutes. Serve.

Serves 4.

Ingredients:

1 *pound of jumbo shrimp*

1 *teaspoon of salt*

1 *stalk of green onion*

1 *tablespoon of ginger slices*

2 *small hot peppers*

Orange and Ginger Flavored Shrimp in Tomato Sauce

Therapeutic Uses: Clears excessive heat from the body. Treats fever and cough. Nourishes the stomach and stimulates appetite. Helps to treat diabetes and stomach or kidney deficiencies.

Ingredents:

- 1 pound of shrimp
- 2 cups of tomato sauce
- 1 teaspoon of salt
- 2 tablespoons of cooking wine
- 2 teaspoons of vinegar
- 2 teaspoons of sugar
- 1/3 cup of dried tangerine peels
- 1/2 tablespoon of ginger slices
- 1 tablespoon of green onion pieces
- 2 tablespoons of vegetable oil

Directions:

1. Clean shrimp and rinse.
2. Soak dried tangerine peels in warm water for 5 minutes.
3. Heat vegetable oil in wok over high heat; then stir-fry green onion and ginger for 15 seconds.
4. Slide in shrimp and stir-fry for 10 minutes, until they turn pink.
5. Add in tomato sauce, soaked tangerine peels, salt, cooking wine, sugar, vinegar and 2 cups of water.
6. When it boils, reduce to low heat and simmer for 10 minutes.
7. Increase to high heat for 3 minutes to evaporate the sauce in the wok.
8. Discard tangerine peels, green onion and ginger.
9. Transfer shrimp to a plate. Serve.

Serves 5.

A TIP FROM THE MASTER

Tangerine peels can be purchased in most Asian grocery stores or you can dry your own.

Shrimp with Chives

Therapeutic Uses: Invigorates the kidney. Reverses calcium deficiency. Treats osteoporosis. Cleans the stomach and intestines to improve digestion.

Directions:

1. Wash chives and cut into 1-inch strips.
2. Place chive tips and leaves on separate plates.
3. Wash dried shrimp and drain completely.
4. Heat vegetable oil in wok over high heat; then slide in shrimp and stir-fry for 10 seconds.
5. Slide in chive tips and stir-fry for 3 minutes.
6. Add in chive leaves and stir-fry for 2 minutes.
7. Add in salt and mix well. Serve.

Serves 3.

Ingredients:

1 cup of dried shrimp

1/3 pound of chives

3 tablespoons of vegetable oil

1/2 teaspoon of salt

A TIP FROM THE MASTER

Since shrimp are high in cholesterol those watching their cholesterol should avoid eating shrimp dishes.

Steamed Mandarin Fish with Garlic

Therapeutic Uses: Replenishes proteins in the body. Nourishes the spleen and stomach. Relieves fatigue due to overworking of the spleen. Helps to treat tuberculosis.

Ingredients:

- 1 pound of Mandarin fish
- 4 cloves of garlic (purple-peel garlic is preferable.)
- 1/2 teaspoon of salt
- 2 tablespoons of cooking wine

Directions:

1. Scale fish, remove gills and internal organs. Rinse and drain.
2. Remove garlic peels. Insert one piece into fish mouth and put the rest into fish belly.
3. Put fish on a large plate. Sprinkle cooking wine and salt in and on the fish.
4. Place the plate on a rack in a steaming pot over high heat and steam for 40 minutes. Serve.

Serves 4.

Steamed Eel With Ginger

Therapeutic Uses: Combats fatigue. Treats deficiencies in calcium, protein, and phosphorus. Helps patients recover from tuberculosis if dish is consumed regularly. Fights deterioration and weakness during convalescence.

Directions:

1. Clean eel, removing internal organs. Rinse and cut into 2-inch sections.
2. Put eel sections on a plate, sprinkle on salt and cooking wine, and place ginger slices on top.
3. Put the plate on a steaming rack in a pot with water over high heat. Cover, but leave space for air to escape and avoid overflow. Steam for 1 hour.
4. Transfer to new plate. Serve.

Serves 5.

Ingredients:

2 pounds of fresh eel

1 teaspoon of salt

2 tablespoons of cooking wine

3 slices of ginger

A TIP FROM THE MASTER

Ask wherever you purchase your fresh eel if they can clean it for you. If they cannot, or if you just prefer to give it a try yourself, you will need a couple of supplies: a sharp knife, a clean kitchen towel, and a clean pair of pliers. Eel tends to be slippery so use the kitchen towel to hold the fish on a solid cutting surface. Make a cut around the neck and you will see that the thick skin separates from the flesh of the fish. Grab the skin with the pliers and pull down the length of the body until you reach the tail. Cut the skin free and discard it. Now slice open the stomach and remove the innards, cut off the head, and rinse the cleaned eel under cold water. The fish is now ready to slice for cooking.

Butterfish With Garlic

Therapeutic Uses: Replenishes protein in the body. Acts as a tonic for the kidney and liver. Improves vision. Nourishes the brain. Replenishes the spleen. Improves appetite. Removes toxins. Treats obesity, hypertension, indigestion, worms, edema, diabetes and acute chronic epidemic diseases like dysentery, inflammation of the intestines, typhoid fever, and the flu.

Ingredients:

1 pound of butterfish

1 1/2 tablespoons of garlic

2 tablespoons of soy sauce

2 tablespoons of cooking wine

1 tablespoon of vinegar

1/2 teaspoon of salt

1 teaspoon of sugar

1 tablespoon of chopped green onion

1/2 teaspoon of chopped ginger

1/2 teaspoon of chopped garlic

2 1/2 tablespoons of vegetable oil

2 cups of water

Directions:

1. Scale the fish, remove its internal organs, and rinse completely.
2. Cut the fish diagonally on two sides. Each cut should be 1/3-inch deep. There are a total 4 cuts on each side, with a half-inch space between two cuts.
3. Paint the fish with 1 tablespoon of soy sauce, half of the salt and 1 tablespoon of cooking wine. Let stand for 10 minutes.
4. Heat vegetable oil in wok over high heat, then slide in fish and fry until it turns golden brown on both sides.

Butterfish with Garlic, continued

5. Remove and drain the fish. Transfer to a plate and let stand.

6. Leave about two tablespoons of vegetable oil in the wok over high heat. Add ginger, garlic and green onions, and stir-fry for 20 seconds.

7. Slide in fish, remaining soy sauce, remaining cooking wine, vinegar, remaining salt, sugar and 2 cups of water.

8. Lower heat, cover wok and simmer for 20 minutes.

9. Turn the fish over twice during simmering. Serve.

Serves 4.

A TIP FROM THE MASTER

The butterfish, also known as dollar fish and Pacific Pompano, has a tender texture and sweet flavor.

Twice Cooked Belt Fish

Therapeutic Uses: Replenishes protein in the body. Nourishes the kidney and brain. Calms the liver. Relieves chronic fatigue. Treats loin and knee pain due to kidney deficiencies.

Ingredients:

1 pound of belt fish

2 tablespoons of soy sauce

1 tablespoon of sesame oil

5 tablespoons of vegetable oil

1/2 teaspoon of salt

1 tablespoon of chopped green onion

1/2 tablespoon of ginger slices

1 tablespoon of coriander pieces

2 cups of chicken broth (or water)

Directions:

1. Scale the fish, cut and discard its head, and remove its internal organs. Rinse and drain.
2. Cut fish into 2-inch segments.
3. Heat vegetable oil in wok over medium heat; then slide in fish segments and fry until both sides turn golden brown.
4. Transfer to a large bowl.
5. Add salt, green onions and ginger. Then pour in 2 cups of chicken broth (or water).
6. Put the bowl on a steamer rack in a large soup pot with water over high heat. Steam for a half hour, until fish is cooked.
7. Carefully remove the bowl, sprinkle sesame oil and coriander pieces over the fish.

Serves 4.

A TIP FROM THE MASTER

This dish is high in cholesterol content and may be unhealthy for those suffering from cardiovascular diseases. The beltfish is a native of the Eastern China Sea. It is an eel-like fish that is normally imported. You can purchase beltfish in Asian food markets and fish markets.

Crisp Kelp

Therapeutic Uses: Replenishes the blood. Removes congestion and other blockages (stasis) in the body. Clears vessels. Removes excess heat from the body. Facilitates the circulation of body fluids. Treats cardiovascular diseases and diabetes.

Directions:

1. Wash the soaked kelp and cut into triangular pieces.
2. Combine wheat flour with 1 1/2 cups of water.
3. Coat each kelp piece with flour by dipping it.
4. Heat vegetable oil in wok over high heat; then slide in kelp pieces and deep-fry until brown. Transfer and let stand.
5. Make sauce by mixing soy sauce, vinegar, salt, sugar, cooking wine and garlic pieces
6. Remove oil from wok leaving only 2 tablespoons.
7. Pour in the sauce and cook until boiling.
8. Slide in fried kelp. Stir to mix several times. Serve.

Serves 2.

Ingredients:

1/3 pound of soaked kelp

3 cups of vegetable oil

2 tablespoons of starch

2 tablespoons of raw sugar

2 teaspoons of vinegar

2 tablespoons of cooking wine

1 cup of wheat flour

1 tablespoon of soy sauce

1/2 teaspoon of salt

1/2 tablespoon of garlic pieces

1 1/2 cups of water

A TIP FROM THE MASTER

Kelp is a healthy versatile sea vegetable. Sea vegetables are packed with minerals and chlorophyll. When soaked in warm water dry kelp expands by about 40%, absorbing up to five times its weight.

Stir-Fried Salmon

Therapeutic Uses: Nourishes the kidney and brain. Improves vision. Replenishes the protein needed by the human body. Helps in the absorption of calcium. Treats obesity, hypertension, and diabetes.

Ingredients:

1 pound of salmon fillet

2 cups of vegetable oil

3 tablespoons of cooking wine

2 tablespoons of soy sauce

1 tablespoon of raw sugar

1/4 cup of green onion strips (each about an inch long)

1/2 tablespoon of ginger strips

2 cups of water

Directions:

1. Cut salmon fillet into 5-inch x 2-inch strips.
2. Cover strips in soy sauce and let stand for 10 minutes.
3. Heat vegetable oil in wok over high heat; then slide in salmon and deep-fry until fillet turns golden brown.
4. Remove and let stand for 10 minutes.
5. Remove vegetable oil from wok, leaving only 2 tablespoons in the wok.
6. Slide in green onion and ginger strips and stir-fry for 1 minute.
7. Add water, sugar, cooking wine, and salt. Mix well.
8. Slide in fried salmon strips, reduce the heat and simmer for 8-10 minutes. Serve.

Serves 4.

Inkfish with Garlic and Chives

Therapeutic Uses: Increases kidney energy. Cleanses stomach, digestive system, and intestines. Treats fatigue due to kidney deficiency and indigestion. Helps to treat hepatitis, hypertension, and diabetes.

Directions:

1. Cut the inkfish into 2-inch pieces.
2. Wash and cut chives into 1-inch strips.
3. Cut garlic into pieces.
4. Heat vegetable oil in wok over high heat; then slide in garlic pieces and stir-fry for 10 minutes.
5. Slide in inkfish strips and stir-fry for 1 minute.
6. Add in chive strips and stir-fry for 5 minutes.
7. Add in salt and soy sauce and mix well for 30 seconds. Serve.

Serves 2.

Ingredients:

1/2 pound of inkfish

1/2 pound of chives

2 cloves of garlic

1/2 tablespoon of soy sauce

1/2 teaspoon of salt

3 tablespoons of vegetable oil

A TIP FROM THE MASTER

Inkfish is a type of squid or calamari. It can be found in many fish and seafood markets as well as in larger Asian markets.

Zesty Mustard Squid Strips

Therapeutic Uses: Stimulates appetite. Replenishes energy. Facilitates the circulation of body fluid to relieve swelling. Treats hypertension and diabetes.

Ingredients:

1/2 pound of squid

1 tablespoon of mustard

1 teaspoon of garlic pieces

1 tablespoon of vinegar

1/2 tablespoon of raw sugar

1/2 teaspoon of salt

1 tablespoon of sesame oil

Directions:

1. Cut squid into 1 1/2-inch pieces and boil in water for 5 minutes.
2. Transfer to a plate and let stand.
3. Make sauce by mixing garlic, mustard, vinegar, sugar, salt, and sesame oil.
4. Pour the sauce over squid strips. Mix well and let stand for 15 minutes. Serve.

Serves 3.

A TIP FROM THE MASTER

For best results use only fresh squid (calamari) and be sure not to overcook.

Eel with Pickled Cucumber

Therapeutic Uses: Reduces fatigue. Removes dampness and gas in the body. Facilitates blood circulation and reduces blood-sugar levels. Treats rheumatic arthritis, diabetes and poor appetite due to spleen and stomach deficiencies.

Directions:

1. Clean the eel to remove and discard all internal organs.
2. Apply salt inside and outside. Let it stand for 10 minutes.
3. Heat vegetable oil in wok over high heat; then slide in eel and deep-fry for 8 minutes, until eel turns brown.
4. Transfer the eel to a plate and place pickled cucumber pieces around it. Serve.

Serves 3.

Ingredients:

1 pound of fresh eel

10 pieces of pickled cucumber

1 teaspoon of salt

1 1/2 cups of vegetable oil

A TIP FROM THE MASTER

Eel can be purchased in many seafood and fish markets, as well as some Asian grocery stores. For advice on cleaning an eel at home see my tip on page 114.

Perch with Mushroom

Therapeutic Uses: Nourishes the kidney and brain. Improves vision. Provides needed protein. Helps with the absorption of calcium. Treats obesity, hypertension, and diabetes.

Ingredients:

1 pound of perch

1 cup of mushrooms

1 teaspoon of salt

2 tablespoons of soy sauce

1 stalk of green onion

1/2 tablespoon of pepper

2 tablespoons of sesame oil

2 eggs

4 tablespoons of vegetable oil

2 tablespoons of cooking wine

Directions:

1. Clean perch and cut into thin slices. Cut mushrooms into slices. Cut green onion into 1-inch chunks.
2. Heat 2 tablespoons of vegetable oil in wok, add green onions, stir-fry for 15 seconds, then add salt, soy sauce, pepper, sesame oil, cooking wine and starch. Mix well to make sauce.
3. Separate eggs and discard yolks. Beat egg whites. Put the perch slices into the egg white.
4. Heat remaining vegetable oil in the wok, add mushroom, perch slices, and egg and stir-fry for 3 minutes.
5. Pour the sauce made in step 2 into the wok. Go on stir-frying for 1 minute. Serve.

Serves 4.

Sautéed Trout

Therapeutic Uses: Nourishes the kidney and brain. Improves vision. Restores depleted protein. Helps promote calcium absorption. Treats obesity, hypertension, and diabetes.

Directions:

1. Clean the trout, spread salt inside and outside, and let stand for 10 minutes.
2. Cut green onion into half-inch chunks.
3. Make sauce by mixing sugar, soy sauce, vinegar, cooking wine and a half-cup of water.
4. Heat 3 tablespoons of vegetable oil in wok over high heat; then slide in trout and fry until both sides turn golden brown. Remove from wok.
5. Add the remaining oil to wok, then slide in green onions and ginger slices and stir-fry for 10 seconds.
6. Pour in the sauce from step two.
7. Slide the trout into wok, reduce heat to medium and simmer for 8 minutes. Serve.

Ingredients:

1 pound of trout

2 tablespoons of soy sauce

1/2 teaspoon of salt

1 stalk of green onion

1/2 tablespoon of ginger slices

1 tablespoon of vinegar

2 tablespoons of cooking wine

1 tablespoon of sugar

4 tablespoons of vegetable oil

1/2 cup of water

Serves 4.

Curried Fish with Onions

Therapeutic Uses: Nourishes the kidney, brain, stomach, and spleen. Improves vision. Stimulates appetite. Replaces depleted protein. Helps in the absorption of calcium. Treats obesity, hypertension, and diabetes.

Ingredients:

1 pound of any fish fillet

1 1/2 cups of cooking wine

2 tablespoons of curry powder

1/5 cup of onions slices

1 teaspoon of salt

3 tablespoons of vegetable oil

Directions:

1. Cut onion into slices.
2. Marinade fillet into cooking wine for 5 minutes.
3. Heat 2 tablespoons of vegetable oil in wok over high heat; then slide in fish fillet and fry until golden brown.
4. Remove fish and let stand.
5. Add remaining vegetable oil to wok; then slide in onion slices and stir-fry for 2 minutes.
6. Add curry powder, 1 cup of water and salt to wok.
7. After it boils, remove and pour the sauce over the fish fillets on the plate. Serve.

Serves 3.

A TIP FROM THE MASTER

In general, seafood is considered to have a yang quality. However, some fish are more yang than some and some fish have more of a yin quality than others. For example the darker the fish is, take tuna for instance, the more yang it is said to be and the oilier the fish, like salmon or mackerel, the more yin it is considered to be.

Fish Fillet with Asparagus

Therapeutic Uses: Nourishes the kidney and brain. Improves vision. Replenishes protein in the body. Helps in the absorption of calcium. Clears away excessive body heat. Facilitates the production of body fluid to remove swelling. Treats obesity, hypertension, and diabetes.

Directions:

1. Cut fish fillet into 1-inch squares.
2. Cut asparagus into 1-inch pieces.
3. Cut green onion into 1-inch chunks.
4. Dissolve starch in a half-cup of water.
5. Separate yolk from eggs and beat egg white only.
6. Combine fish fillet with egg whites.
7. Heat vegetable oil in wok over high heat; then slide in fish fillet and deep fry for about 40 seconds.
8. Remove fish from wok, drain off excess oil and let stand.
9. Remove oil from wok, leaving only 2 tablespoons in wok.
10. Add in ginger, garlic, and green onion and stir-fry for 15 seconds.
11. Slide in asparagus pieces and stir-fry for 2 minutes.
12. Add in salt, cooking wine, and 1 cup of water.
13. When mixture in wok boils, pour in dissolved starch. Stir several times to thicken sauce.
14. Slide in fish fillets again and mix well with sauce in wok. Serve.

Serves 3.

Ingredients:

1/2 pound of any fish fillet

1/2 pound of asparagus

2 cups of vegetable oil

2 tablespoons of cooking wine

2 tablespoons of starch

2 eggs

1 stalk of green onion

1/2 tablespoon of ginger slices

1/2 tablespoon of garlic pieces

1/2 teaspoon of salt

Sautéed Codfish

Therapeutic Uses: Nourishes the kidney and brain. Improves vision. Replenishes protein in the body. Helps the body absorb needed calcium. Treats obesity, hypertension and diabetes.

Ingredients:

1 pound of codfish

2 cups of vegetable oil

3 tablespoons of cooking wine

2 tablespoons of soy sauce

1 tablespoon of raw sugar

1/2 tablespoon of green onion pieces

1/2 tablespoon of ginger strips

1/3 teaspoon of salt

2 cups of water

Directions:

1. Clean codfish to remove internal organs.
2. Coat fish in soy sauce inside and out. Let it stand for 10 minutes.
3. Heat vegetable oil in wok over high heat; then slide in fish and deep-fry until it turns golden brown. Remove fish.
4. Remove vegetable oil, leaving only 1 tablespoon in the wok.
5. Slide in green onion and ginger strips to stir-fry for 1 minute. Put in 2 cups of water, sugar, cooking wine, and salt. Mix well.
6. When the sauce in wok is boiling, slide in fried fish again. Reduce to low heat and simmer for 10 minutes. Serve.

Serves 3.

Crucian With Green Onion and Coriander

Therapeutic Uses: Facilitates the passage of body fluids. Nourishes the stomach, liver and brain. Facilitates milk production in women after delivery. Reduces swelling. Treats hepatitis, hypertension, and diabetes.

Ingredients:

1 pound of crucian carp

2 stalks of green onion

1 cup of fresh coriander

1 teaspoon of salt

2 tablespoons of soy sauce

2 tablespoons of vegetable oil

Directions:

1. Clean the fish and remove its head and tail.
2. Cut green onions into 2-inch pieces.
3. Cut coriander into 1-inch strips.
4. Boil fish in water with half of the salt for 10 minutes.
5. Remove fish and sprinkle remaining salt on both sides; then put it on a plate.
6. Add green onions and coriander and pour soy sauce on the fish.
7. Heat vegetable oil in wok over high heat; sprinkle the hot oil over the fish. Serve.

Serves 4.

Fish Fillet with Garlic and Ginger Cucumbers

Therapeutic Uses: Nourishes the kidney and brain. Improves vision. Provides needed protein. Helps the absorption of calcium. Clears away excessive heat in the body. Facilitates the circulation of body fluid. Removes toxins from the body. Treats obesity, hypertension, cancer, and diabetes.

Ingredients:

- 1 pound of any fish fillet
- 1 cucumber
- 2 cups of vegetable oil
- 2 tablespoons of cooking wine
- 2 tablespoons of starch
- 2 eggs
- 1 stalk of green onion
- 1/2 tablespoon of ginger pieces
- 1/2 tablespoon of garlic pieces
- 1/2 teaspoon of salt
- 1 cup of water

Directions:

1. Cut fish fillet into 1-inch squares.
2. Cut cucumber into 1-inch slices.
3. Cut green onion into 1-inch strips.
4. Dissolve starch in 1/2 cup of water.
5. Separate egg whites from yolk. Discard yolk and beat egg whites.
6. Combine fish fillet with egg whites.
7. Heat vegetable oil in wok over high heat; then slide in fish fillet and deep fry for about 40 seconds or until each piece floats on oil surface. Remove fish and drain oil.
8. Remove oil from wok, leaving only 2 tablespoons in wok.
9. Add in ginger, garlic, and green onion and stir-fry quickly for 15 seconds.
10. Slide in cucumber pieces and stir-fry for 2 minutes.
11. Add in salt, cooking wine, and 1 cup of water.
12. When mixture boils, pour in dissolved starch. Stir several times to make sauce thicker.
13. Slide fish fillets into wok again and mix well with sauce. Serve.

Serves 4.

Spicy Sautéed Conch

Therapeutic Uses: Nourishes the kidney and brain. Improves vision. Provides needed protein. Helps in the absorption of calcium. Treats obesity, hypertension, and diabetes.

Directions:

1. Slice the conch meat and boil in water for 10 minutes.
2. Remove fish, drain, and allow to cool.
3. Make sauce by mixing pepper oil, sesame oil, soy sauce, salt, pepper and chopped green onions.
4. Pour the sauce over the conch slices and mix evenly. Serve.

Serves 3.

Ingredients:

1/2 pound of conch meat

1 tablespoon of pepper oil

3 tablespoons of sesame oil

2 tablespoons of soy sauce

1/4 teaspoon of salt

1/2 teaspoon of pepper

1 tablespoon of green onion pieces

A TIP FROM THE MASTER

Conch (pronounced 'konk') is a type of marine snail or mollusk. Conch meat has a mildly sweet flavor that is often described as clam-like in taste. You can purchase conch in many fish and seafood markets as well as some Asian food markets.

Sweet and Sour Crisp-skin Crucian Fish

あで

Therapeutic Uses: Facilitates milk production in women after birth. Treats hepatitis, swelling, hypertension, and diabetes.

Ingredients:

1 pound of crucian fish

2 tablespoons of raw sugar

1 teaspoon of vinegar

4 tablespoons of cooking wine

2 tablespoons of soy sauce

2 tablespoons of starch

2 stalks of green onion

1 tablespoon of ginger strips

1 teaspoon of garlic

1 teaspoon of salt

1 cup of maize flour

1 cup of vegetable oil

Directions:

1. Clean the fish and make 3 cuts on each side.
2. Smear 1/2 teaspoon of salt over the fish and let stand for 10 minutes.
3. Combine maize flour with 1 cup of water and mix well.
4. Dip the fish into the mixture and coat completely. Set aside.
5. Cut green onion into 1-inch strips.
6. Make sauce by mixing sugar, vinegar, soy sauce, cooking wine, remaining salt and starch.
7. Heat vegetable oil in wok over high heat; then slide in fish coated with flour and deep-fry for 8 minutes, until it turns golden brown.
8. Transfer fish to a plate.
9. Drain oil from wok, leaving only 2–3 tablespoons.
10. Slide in ginger, garlic, and green onion and stir-fry for 10 seconds.
11. Pour in the sauce from step 6 and cook for 3 minutes.
12. Pour the hot sauce over the fish. Serve.

Serves 3.

Gingered Carp

Therapeutic Uses: Facilitates the passage of body fluids. Nourishes the stomach, liver, and brain. Provides necessary protein. Reverses poor appetite caused by stomach and spleen deficiencies. Helps to treat hepatitis. Helps to treat hypertension.

Directions:

1. Clean the fish and make 3 cuts on each side.
2. Cut green onion into 1-inch strips.
3. Boil fish in water for 5 minutes. Remove and drain.
4. Smear 1/2 teaspoon of salt and 1 tablespoon of cooking wine on fish. Let fish stand for 10 minutes.
5. Place fish on a plate and put green onions and ginger on its back.
6. Put the plate on a steamer rack in a pot with water and steam it over high heat for 10 minutes.
7. Remove the plate carefully. Keep the ginger and green onions.
8. Chop the ginger into bits; then mix with vinegar, sesame oil, remaining salt, and soy sauce.
9. Pour the sauce over the steamed fish. Serve.

Serves 3.

Ingredients:

- 1 pound of carp fish
- 1 tablespoon of fresh ginger
- 1 tablespoon of vinegar
- 2 tablespoons of sesame oil
- 2 tablespoons of soy sauce
- 1 teaspoon of salt
- 2 tablespoons of cooking wine
- 1 stalk of green onion
- 1 teaspoon of ginger slices

A TIP FROM THE MASTER

This dish should be avoided if you have a cough with congestion.

Jellyfish and Turnip あ

Therapeutic Uses: Invigorates the stomach to improve digestion. Helps the lungs to clear congestion. Reduces blood pressure. Facilitates the circulation of body fluid. Treats hypertension, stomach burn, enlargement of the thyroid gland due to iodine shortage, and chronic bronchitis.

Ingredients:

- 1/2 pound of jellyfish
- 1/2 pound of turnips
- 3 1/2 teaspoons of salt
- 1/2 cup of soy sauce
- 3 tablespoons of raw sugar
- 1/2 cup of vinegar
- 3 tablespoons of sesame oil
- 1 tablespoon of green onion bits

Directions:

1. Wash and shave turnips.
2. Cut turnips into thin slices, combine with 1/2 teaspoon of salt, mix well and let stand in the refrigerator for one day.
3. Wash jellyfish; then immerse in water mixed with 3 teaspoons of salt for 3 hours.
4. Rewash and drain fish.
5. Place fish in hot water and soak for 10 minutes.
6. Cut jellyfish into thick strips.
7. Rinse fish again with cold water. Drain and let stand.
8. Drain off saltwater from turnip.
9. Mix turnip with jellyfish strips.
10. Mix soy sauce, raw sugar, vinegar, sesame oil, and green onion pieces. Pour sauce over the turnips and fish and mix well. Serve.

Serves 3.

A TIP FROM THE MASTER

Like sashimi and some sushi this is a non-cook dish and the fish is served raw. The dish may not be suitable for everyone. Fresh jellyfish can be found in many Asian markets, fish markets, and seafood stores.

Turnip With Shrimp

Therapeutic Uses: Facilitates the circulation of body fluid. Nourishes the kidney. Treats loin and knee pain due to kidney deficiency. Strengthens bones and muscles. Helps to treat osteoporosis.

Directions:

1. Clean turnips and cut into 1/2-inch cubes.
2. Wash dried shrimp and drain.
3. Boil turnip cubes in water for 5 minutes.
4. Remove turnips and let cool.
5. Heat vegetable oil in wok over high heat; then slide in shrimp and green-onions, followed by turnip cubes. Stir-fry for 3 minutes.
6. Add in sugar, salt, soy sauce, and a cup of warm water. Reduce to low heat and simmer for 7 minutes.
7. Dissolve starch in a tablespoon of water and pour over the turnip cubes in the wok. Mix well. Serve.

Serves 3.

Ingredients:

1 pound of turnips

1/2 cup of dried small shrimp

2 tablespoons of vegetable oil

1 tablespoon of starch

2 tablespoons of soy sauce

1/2 teaspoon of salt

1/2 tablespoon of raw sugar

1/2 tablespoon of green onions

1 cup of warm water

A TIP FROM THE MASTER

Shrimp are high in cholesterol and those watching their cholesterol levels may want to limit the amount of shrimp they eat.

Shrimp With Tomato Sauce

Therapeutic Uses: Nourishes the stomach and spleen. Reverses poor appetite due to stomach ailments such as ulcers.

Ingredients:

1/2 pound of cleaned shrimp

2 tablespoons of tomato sauce

1 egg

2 tablespoons of vegetable oil

1 teaspoon of raw sugar

1 teaspoon of salt

1 cup of snow peas

2 tablespoons of starch

1 tablespoon of cooking wine

1/2 tablespoon of sesame oil

1 cup of water

Directions:

1. Clean shrimp and put them in a bowl. Beat in egg and add half the salt and 1 tablespoon of starch. Mix well.
2. Heat 1 tablespoon of vegetable oil in the wok over high heat; then slide in shrimp mixture and fry until golden.
3. Transfer to a plate and let stand.
4. Put remaining oil in wok and heat over medium heat; then slide in tomato sauce and snow peas and stir-fry for 2 minutes.
5. Add in cooking wine, sugar, remaining salt, and 1 cup of water.
6. When it boils, add in remaining starch.
7. Slide in shrimp and stir several times.
8. Remove, sprinkle sesame oil on it, and serve.

Serves 3.

Sweet and Sour Yellow Croaker あので

Therapeutic Uses: Improves appetite. Nourishes the liver. Helps treat hepatitis, especially during the recovery period. Treats hypertension, diabetes, and high cholesterol.

Directions:

1. Scale the yellow croaker and remove gills. Remove internal organs through gills. Cut out dorsal fin. Wash croaker and put in a bowl. Pour 2 teaspoons of soy sauce over it and let stand.
2. Cut garlic sprout into 1-inch strips. Cut tofu into half-inch cubes.
3. Heat 2 tablespoons of vegetable oil in wok over high heat; then slide in croaker and fry until golden. Transfer to a plate and let stand.
4. Heat remaining vegetable oil in wok over high heat; then slide in ginger and green onions and stir-fry quickly for 10 seconds.
5. Slide croaker back into wok; then combine with cooking wine, raw sugar, remaining soy sauce and 2 cups of water. When it boils, reduce heat and simmer for 10 minutes.
6. Turn heat up to high; then add in tofu, salt and a cup of water. Cook until it boils.
7. Combine vinegar, pepper, coriander and garlic sprout in a serving bowl. Pour croaker, tofu and sauce mixture into the bowl.

Serves 4.

Ingredients:

1 yellow croaker

1/2 pound of tofu

1 stalk of garlic sprouts

1 cup of fresh coriander

1/2 tablespoon of pepper

1 tablespoon of cooking wine

4 tablespoons of vegetable oil

1 tablespoon of raw sugar

4 tablespoons of vinegar

1/2 tablespoon of ginger strips

1/2 tablespoon of green onion pieces

1 teaspoon of salt

4 teaspoons of soy sauce

3 cups of water

A TIP FROM THE MASTER

When planted, garlic cloves sprout chive-like shoots that can be used as seasoning. You can purchase garlic sprouts in an Asian grocery store or grow your own.

Egg with Shrimp and Spinach

Therapeutic Uses: Facilitates blood circulation. Cleanses the stomach and intestines. Adjusts vital energy. Stops restlessness. Quenches thirst. Lubricates the lungs. Treats constipation and a sense of thirst due to internal dryness. Fights anemia, hypertension, and hemorrhoids.

Ingredients:

2 egg whites

3 tablespoons of dried shrimp

4 cups of spinach

2 teaspoons of soy sauce

2 tablespoons of vegetable oil

2 teaspoons of starch

1 teaspoon of mustard

1 tablespoon of sesame paste

1 tablespoon of vinegar

1/2 tablespoon of garlic

1/2 teaspoon of salt

1 cup of water

Directions:

1. Separate egg whites and yolks. Discard yolks. Beat egg whites in a bowl and whip; then combine with starch and salt. Mix well.
2. Soak dried shrimp in warm water for 5 minutes. Remove and drain.
3. Wash spinach and boil it in water for 3 minutes.
4. Remove spinach and let cool; then cut into 1-inch pieces. Put spinach on a plate.
5. Heat 2 tablespoons of vegetable oil in a pan. Add egg mixture and tilt the pan so the egg completely covers the bottom. Cook over medium heat until the egg is set. Loosen edges and flip the egg to cook the other side.
6. Remove the egg pancake, cut it into strips and put over the spinach.
7. Put shrimp over spinach and egg.
8. Combine mustard and sesame paste with 1 cup of water. Mix well. Then add in soy sauce, garlic and vinegar.
9. Pour the sauce over the spinach. Serve.

Serves 2.

Healing Vegetarian Dishes

Mouthwatering meatless meals
are a staple of the
healing Chinese diet.
The vegetarian dishes I have
chosen to share with you
are not only naturally
low in fat and healthy,
they are satisfying palate
pleasers as well.

Eggs with Chives

Therapeutic Uses: Treats male impotence and premature ejaculation. Fights loin and knee pain and frequent urination caused by a kidney deficiency. Improves digestion.

Ingredients:

1 cup of fresh chives strips

2 eggs

1 tablespoon of vegetable oil

1 teaspoon of salt

Directions:

1. Wash chives and cut into 1-inch strips.
2. Break eggs into a bowl and whip evenly; add half the salt.
3. Heat 1/2 tablespoon vegetable oil in the wok over medium heat; then pour in whipped eggs.
4. When eggs turn solid, remove from wok, break into large pieces, and place in a bowl.
5. Heat remaining oil in wok over high heat; add chive strips and stir-fry for 5 minutes.
6. Add egg pieces to wok.
7. Fry for another 2 minutes; then add the remaining salt. Serve.

Serves 1.

Chinese Cabbage in Vinegar

Therapeutic Uses: Relieves constipation. Treats cough. Treats bleeding of the stomach and intestines. Helps treat obesity.

Directions:

1. Wash and cut cabbage into 1-inch pieces.
2. Chop ginger and green onion into pieces.
3. Put ginger and green onion in a bowl and add in soy sauce, salt, vinegar, cornstarch and 2/3 cup of water. Mix well and let stand.
4. Heat vegetable oil in wok over high heat; then slide in cabbage pieces and stir-fry for 5 minutes.
5. Pour in mixed sauce and stir-fry for another minute, until cabbage and sauce are well mixed. Serve.

Serves 1.

Ingredients:

1 cup of Chinese cabbage

1 tablespoon of soy sauce

1 tablespoon of vinegar

1/4 teaspoon of salt

1/2 tablespoon of green onions

1/4 tablespoon of ginger bits

1 tablespoon of vegetable oil

1 tablespoon of cornstarch

2/3 cup of water

A TIP FROM THE MASTER

Tender and deliciously mild, Chinese cabbage can be purchased in Asian food markets, natural food stores, and a number of mainstream grocery stores.

Sweet and Sour Zesty Cabbage Rolls

あの

Therapeutic Uses: Nourishes the spleen and stomach. Improves appetite. Treats high cholesterol and cardiovascular diseases.

Ingredients:

5 cabbage leaves

3 carrots

1 cup of bamboo shoots

4 pieces of dried red chili pepper

1 stalk of green onion

1 piece of ginger

1 teaspoon of salt

5 teaspoons of vinegar

5 teaspoons of raw sugar

2 tablespoons of vegetable oil

2 cups of water

Directions:

1. Cut carrots and bamboo shoots into strips.
2. Cut green onion and ginger into thick strips.
3. Soak dried red chili in warm water until soft; then remove the seeds and cut into thick strips.
4. Boil cabbage leaves for 1 minute.
5. Transfer to cool water to cool down. Drain.
6. Boil carrot and bamboo-shoot strips for 1 minute. Drain, transfer and let stand.
7. Heat vegetable oil in wok over high heat; then slide in red pepper, ginger and green onions and stir-fry for 15 seconds.
8. Pour in 2 cups of water; then add vinegar, sugar and salt.

Sweet and Sour Zesty Cabbage Rolls, continued

9. Cook until it boils; then transfer the soup to a large bowl to cool down.
10. Soak cooked cabbage leaves in the cooled soup for 30 minutes.
11. Spread cabbage leaves out on a large plate and put carrot and bamboo-shoot strips in the middle of each of the leaves and wrap each leaf into a roll.
12. Cross-cut the rolls into 2-inch pieces. Arrange the cut rolls on a plate and serve.

Serves 2.

A TIP FROM THE MASTER

Both dried and fresh chilies can cause your skin to sting and feel irritated so always use caution when cooking with them. If possible wear rubber gloves when handling the peppers and be sure to wash your hands and surfaces afterwards.

Chinese Cabbage With Mushrooms

あので

Therapeutic Uses: Soothes the stomach and intestines. Facilitates the circulation of body fluid. Treats constipation and intestinal bleeding. Helps to treat hypertension, heart disease, and diabetes.

Ingredients:

- 1/2 pound of Chinese cabbage
- 1/4 pound of mushrooms
- 2 tablespoons of vegetable oil
- 1 teaspoon of salt
- 1 tablespoon of soy sauce
- 2 teaspoons of sesame oil
- 2 tablespoons of cooking wine
- 2 tablespoons of green onions
- 1/2 tablespoon of garlic
- 1/2 tablespoon of ginger strips

Directions:

1. Wash cabbage and cut into 1-inch pieces.
2. Wash mushrooms and cut each into 4 sections.
3. Heat 1 tablespoon of vegetable oil in wok over high heat; then slide in 1 tablespoon of green onions and stir-fry for 10 seconds.
4. Add in cabbage pieces and stir-fry for 3 minutes. Transfer to a plate and let stand.
5. Heat another tablespoon of vegetable oil over high heat; then slide in mushroom pieces and stir-fry for 3 minutes.
6. Add in soy sauce and cooking wine. After mixing well, slide in cabbage pieces and stir-fry for 3 minutes.
7. Drop in remaining green onions, garlic, and ginger. Sprinkle sesame oil. Mix well. Serve.

Serves 3.

A TIP FROM THE MASTER

Chinese cabbage has a delicious mildly sweet flavor and tender texture. You can find the cabbage in Asian food markets, natural food stores, and many mainstream grocery stores as well. If you are having trouble finding Chinese cabbage Bok Choy is an acceptable substitute in most recipes.

Sweet and Sour Sesame Cabbage

Therapeutic Uses: Replenishes calcium in the body.

Ingredients:

1/2 pound of Chinese cabbage heart

2 tablespoons of sesame paste

2 tablespoons of vinegar

2 teaspoons of raw sugar

2 tablespoons of sesame oil

Directions:

1. Clean the cabbage hearts, and cut into 2-inch strips; place them on a plate.
2. Combine sesame paste with sesame oil, mix well, and pour over the cabbage strips.
3. Sprinkle sugar and vinegar over the cabbage strips. Stir to mix evenly. Serve.

Serves 3.

A TIP FROM THE MASTER

Chinese cabbage can be purchased in most Asian food markets, in natural food stores, and in some mainstream grocery stores.

Gingered Spinach

Therapeutic Uses: Facilitates blood circulation. Stimulates the production of stomach fluid. Nourishes the intestines to improve digestion. Treats constipation and excessive thirst due to internal dryness, anemia, hypertension, and hemorrhoids.

Ingredients:

- 1/2 pound of spinach
- 1 tablespoon of ginger juice
- 2 tablespoons of vinegar
- 1 stalk of green onion
- 1/2 teaspoon of salt
- 1/2 tablespoon of cornstarch
- 2 tablespoons of vegetable oil
- 1/2 tablespoon of sesame oil

Directions:

1. Wash spinach and cut it in half down the middle.
2. Cut the green onion into 1-inch chunks.
3. Make sauce by mixing ginger juice, vinegar, salt, cornstarch and a cup of water. Then sprinkle sesame oil over the mixed sauce.
4. Heat vegetable oil in wok over high heat. Slide in green onions and stir-fry for 15 seconds.
5. Slide in spinach and cook for 5 minutes.
6. Pour the sauce over the spinach and continue stir-frying for 1 minute. Serve.

Serves 3.

A TIP FROM THE MASTER

You may purchase bottled ginger juice or make your own. To make ginger juice at home, peel a large slice of fresh ginger, grate it on a hand grater, pack the gratings into a garlic press, and squeeze out the juice.

Wok-fried Tomatoes

Therapeutic Uses: Stimulates appetite. Reverses thirst due to excessive heat inside the body.

Ingredients:

- 2 tomatoes
- 3 eggs
- 1 teaspoon of salt
- 1 tablespoon of green onions
- 1/2 tablespoon of ginger slices
- 1 cup of chicken broth
- 7 tablespoons of cornstarch
- 6 tablespoons of vegetable oil

Directions:

1. Wash tomatoes and cross-cut into quarter-inch-thick slices.
2. Beat and whip eggs.
3. Dissolve a tablespoon of cornstarch in 1 table-spoon of water.
4. Spread remaining dry cornstarch on a flat plate and coat tomato slices with it.
5. Heat 5 tablespoons of vegetable oil in a wok over high heat.
6. Dip tomato slices in egg; then slide into the wok to fry till brown. Transfer to a plate.
7. Heat remaining oil over high heat; then add the ginger and green onion pieces, followed by chicken broth and salt. Then add the dissolved cornstarch to thicken the broth.
8. Pour broth over fried tomato slices. Serve.

Serves 2.

Mushrooms With Garlic

Therapeutic Uses: Nourishes yin energy. Relieves dryness in the body. Reinvigorates the stomach and spleen. Helps to treat aleukia, chronic hepatitis, hypertension, heart disease, diabetes, and cancer.

Ingredients:

- 1 pound of mushrooms
- 2 tablespoons of garlic pieces
- 1 tablespoon of soy sauce
- 10 1/2 cups of water
- 2 tablespoons of cooking wine
- 1/2 tablespoon of pepper
- 1 teaspoon of salt
- 2 tablespoons of cornstarch
- 2 tablespoons of vegetable oil

Directions:

1. Clean mushrooms and cut into slices.
2. Put a wok with 7 1/2 cups of water over a high heat. When water boils, put in mushroom slices and cook for 3 minutes. Then drain and transfer mushrooms to a plate.
3. Heat vegetable oil over high heat. Add in garlic slices, soy sauce, mushroom slices, salt and 3 cups of water. When it boils, reduce to low heat and simmer for 7 minutes.
4. Add in cornstarch and stir quickly to make the sauce in the wok thicker. Serve.

Serves 3.

Egg and Tomato Sauté

Therapeutic Uses: Improves appetite. Quenches thirst due to excess heat. Increases gastric acid. Helps to treat heatstroke, hypertension, and chronic hepatitis.

Ingredients:

- 3 eggs
- 3 tomatoes
- 1 tablespoon of cooking oil
- 1/2 teaspoon of salt
- 1/2 tablespoon of cooking wine
- 1/2 tablespoon of raw sugar

Directions:

1. Scald tomatoes in boiling water to remove peel.
2. Cut tomatoes into thick slices. Put them in a bowl and let stand.
3. Break eggs into a bowl and whip. Add in half the salt and 1/2 tablespoon of cooking wine and mix evenly.
4. Heat cooking oil over high heat. Slide in tomato slices and stir-fry for 2 minutes. Then add the remaining salt and 1/2 tablespoon of sugar.
5. Pour in egg mixture and continue stir-frying for another 2 minutes. Serve.

Serves 2.

A TIP FROM THE MASTER

If you suffer from high cholesterol and/or arthritis you may want to avoid this dish.

Crispy Sweet and Sour Turnip Salad

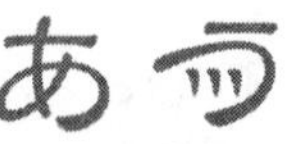

Therapeutic Uses: Helps to cleanse the blood from toxins. Improves blood circulation. Adjusts vital energy to improve digestion. Facilitates fluid passage to remove toxins. Prevents cancer.

Ingredients:

- 1/2 pound of turnips
- 2 teaspoons of raw sugar
- 2 teaspoons of vinegar
- 1 teaspoon of salt
- 1/2 teaspoon of soy sauce
- 1/4 tablespoon of ginger slices
- 1/2 tablespoon of green onions
- 1/2 tablespoon of sesame oil

Directions:

1. Peel the turnip and cut into thin slices.
2. Combine salt with turnip slices and let stand for 6 hours.
3. Drain out salt water.
4. Add sugar, vinegar, ginger, green onions, and sesame oil to turnip slices. Mix well.
5. Let stand for another 30 minutes before serving.

Serves 2.

A TIP FROM THE MASTER

This is a delicious non-cook recipe, similar to coleslaw or cucumber salad, which results in a slightly sweet and salty salad with a lot of crunch and just a bit of a warming bite.

Fresh Corn With Hot Green Pepper あで

Therapeutic Uses: Facilitates the production of body fluid to remove swelling. Nourishes the stomach to relieve constipation.Treats indigestion, hypertension and diabetes.

Directions:

1. Wash fresh corn.
2. Wash hot green pepper and cut it diagonally into small strips.
3. Heat a wok over medium heat (no oil in this step); then put in pepper strips and dry-fry for 2 minutes, until the strips shrink. Remove and let stand.
4. Heat vegetable oil in wok over high heat. Slide in corn and stir-fry for 3 minutes.
5. Add in pepper strips and go on stir-frying for 2 minutes; then add salt and mix well. Serve.

Serves 3.

Ingredients:

1/2 pound of fresh corn

1 hot green pepper

1/2 teaspoon of salt

3 tablespoons of vegetable oil

Eggs With Cucumber

Therapeutic Uses: Provides essential proteins and vitamins. Clears away heat. Facilitates the circulation of body fluid. Useful for people on a diet.

Ingredients:

2 eggs

1/2 pound of cucumber

1 tablespoon of green onions

2 tablespoons of vegetable oil

1/2 teaspoon of salt

1 tablespoon of starch

Directions:

1. Wash and cut cucumber into small pieces.
2. Dissolve starch in 1/2 cup of water.
3. Beat and whip eggs in a bowl.
4. Heat 1 tablespoon of vegetable oil in wok over medium heat. Add in egg and stir-fry until it sets.
5. Slice egg into 1-inch pieces. Remove and let stand.
6. Heat remaining oil over high heat; then slide in cucumber pieces and stir-fry for 2 minutes.
7. Add in egg pieces, green onions and melted starch.
8. Add in salt and stir-fry for 1 minute. Serve.

Serves 2.

Crisp and Hot Cucumber Strips

Therapeutic Uses: Clears away excessive body heat. Facilitates the circulation of body fluid. Removes toxins. Helps reduce throat swelling, pain, thirst, and vomiting due to pathogenic heat. Helps to treat obesity and diabetes.

Ingredients:

- 2 cucumbers
- 1 tablespoon of soy sauce
- 1 tablespoon of vegetable oil
- 1/2 teaspoon of salt
- 1/2 teaspoon of sugar
- 1 piece of hot red chili

Directions:

1. Wash cucumbers and cut in half. Remove seeds; then cut into 2-inch chunks.
2. Combine with salt to stand for 1 hour. Drain off salt water.
3. Heat vegetable oil in wok over medium heat; then slide in red chili to fry for 10 seconds, until it browns.
4. Add in cucumber chunks, soy sauce, and sugar.
5. Increase to high heat and stir-fry quickly for 1 minute. Serve.

Serves 2.

A TIP FROM THE MASTER

The longer you cook chili-peppers the hotter the dish you are making will be. A quick-stir fry, like is called for in this dish, adds just a dash of hot flavor. Slowly simmering hot peppers, in a stew for example, will increase the heat level.

Fried Hot-n-Spicy Green Pepper あの

Therapeutic Uses: Stimulates appetite. Helps to reduce blood pressure. Treats cardiovascular diseases.

Ingredients:

- 7 hot green peppers
- 3 tablespoons of vegetable oil
- 2 tablespoons of soy sauce
- 1 tablespoon of raw sugar
- 1 tablespoon of vinegar
- 1/4 teaspoon of salt
- 1/2 tablespoon of green onions

Directions:

1. Wash and drain hot green peppers.
2. Make sauce by combining soy sauce, vinegar, sugar, salt and green onions. Mix well and let stand.
3. Heat vegetable oil in wok over medium heat; then slide in peppers and fry until brown (there should be bubbles on the surface.)
4. Pour the sauce over peppers.
5. Reduce to low heat, cover the wok and let simmer for 1 minute. Serve.

Serves 2.

A TIP FROM THE MASTER

People with stomach or intestinal problems should avoid this dish.

Avocado and Tofu With Tomato Salad

Therapeutic Uses: Lubricates the intestines. Treats obesity, constipation, weak stomach, and weak intestines.

Ingredients:

1 avocado

1/3 pound of tofu

3 tomatoes

2 cloves of garlic

1/2 tablespoon of basil

2 tablespoons of olive oil

2 tablespoons of soy sauce

Directions:

1. Peel avocado and cut into 1/3-inch cubes.
2. Wash tomatoes and cut into 1/3-inch cubes.
3. Cut tofu into 1/3-inch cubes.
4. Crush garlic and chop into small pieces.
5. Put avocado, tofu, and tomato cubes in a bowl. Sprinkle on soy sauce, basil, and olive oil. Serve.

Serves 2.

Bitter Melon with Soybeans

Therapeutic Uses: Helps to reduce blood pressure. Calms the gall bladder. Treats asthma, insomnia, and cancer.

Ingredients:

1 pound of bitter melon

1/2 cup of soybeans

1 tablespoon of soy sauce

1 tablespoon of sesame oil

1/2 teaspoon of salt

1/2 tablespoon of vinegar

Directions:

1. Cut each bitter melon in half, remove seeds, and chop melon into slices.
2. Boil bitter melon pieces in water for 2 minutes.
3. Remove and let stand on a plate.
4. Boil soybeans in water for 15 minutes, until done.
5. Remove soybeans and place on bitter melon.
6. Sprinkle soy sauce, sesame oil, salt, and vinegar on top. Serve.

Serves 4.

A TIP FROM THE MASTER

Bitter melon—a relative of the squash—resembles a cucumber, but has a bumpier surface. The gourd can be purchased in most Asian and natural food stores.

Sesame Spinach

Therapeutic Uses: Treats hypertension and diabetes. Useful for treating obesity.

Directions:

1. Wash spinach and cut into 2-inch strips.
2. Crush garlic and chop into thin pieces.
3. Boil spinach in water for 2 minutes. Remove and drain.
4. Sprinkle on sesame seeds, soy sauce, vinegar, and garlic. Serve.

Serves 4.

Ingredients:

1/2 pound of spinach

1 tablespoon of sesame seeds

2 teaspoons of soy sauce

1/2 teaspoon of salt

1 clove of garlic

1 teaspoon of vinegar

Bitter Melon with Hot Red Chili Peppers

あで

Therapeutic Uses: Calms the liver. Nourishes the gall bladder. Improves vision. Treats hypertension, diabetes and high cholesterol.

Ingredients:

1/2 pound of bitter melon

3 pieces of hot red chili peppers

1 tablespoon of olive oil

1/2 teaspoon of salt

1 clove of garlic

Directions:

1. Cut each bitter melon in half and remove the seeds; then chop into slices.
2. Crush garlic and chop into bits.
3. Heat olive oil over high heat; slide in red chili peppers and garlic and stir-fry for 5 seconds, until you can smell their fragrance.
4. Slide in bitter-melon and stir-fry for 3 minutes.
5. Add in salt, stir, and mix well. Serve.

Serves 3.

A TIP FROM THE MASTER

As a general rule the smaller and thinner a pepper is the hotter it will be. Bitter melon, a relative of the cucumber, can be purchased in most Asian food markets.

Sweet and Sour Cucumbers

Therapeutic Uses: Harmonizes blood vessels. Helps to cleanse blood from toxins. Improves digestion. Clears away heat and toxins in the body. Helps to reduce cholesterol. Helps to treat hypertension, heart disease, and obesity.

Ingredients:

2 fresh cucumbers

2 tablespoons of vinegar

1 tablespoon of raw sugar

1 teaspoon of salt

1 tablespoon of soy sauce

1/2 tablespoon of mashed garlic

1 tablespoon of sesame oil

Directions:

1. Wash cucumber; then cut off and discard two ends.
2. Cut cucumber into thin slices and put them into a bowl.
3. Add water to cover cucumbers and mix in salt. Let stand for 2 hours.
4. Drain off salt water from cucumber slices.
5. Add vinegar, sugar, mashed garlic, soy sauce, and sesame oil. Serve.

Serves 2.

Cucumber With Garlic

Therapeutic Uses: Harmonizes the blood vessels. Disperses blood stasis (poor blood circulation). Improves digestion. Clears away heat and toxins from the body. Helps to reduce cholesterol and high blood pressure. Helps to treat diabetes and obesity.

Ingredients:

3 cucumbers

1 1/2 tablespoons of garlic

1 teaspoon of salt

2 tablespoons of sesame oil

2 tablespoons of vinegar

Directions:

1. Wash cucumbers; then slice in half along their middles.
2. Cut into cubes. Set cubes on a plate and let stand.
3. Chop garlic into thin pieces. Combine with salt, sesame, and vinegar. Mix well.
4. Pour the sauce over the cucumbers. Serve.

Serves 4.

Cucumber with Coriander and Hot Green Pepper

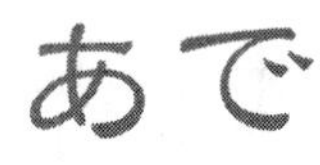

Therapeutic Uses: Facilitates the natural functioning of the stomach and intestine. Stimulates poor appetite caused by heat inside the body due to stomach and spleen deficiencies. Treats hypertension, diabetes, and sickness related to excessive greasy food consumption.

Ingredients:

1 cup of fresh coriander

2 cucumbers

3 hot green peppers

1/2 teaspoon of salt

2 tablespoons of sesame oil

Directions:

1. Cut coriander into pieces.
2. Cut cucumber and hot green pepper into small pieces.
3. Mix coriander, cucumber, and pepper. Sprinkle on salt and sesame oil. Serve.

Serves 3.

A TIP FROM THE MASTER

It is fairly well known that Chili peppers are high in vitamin A and C and are powerful antioxidants. However, there are some lesser known therapeutic uses for chili-peppers. For example, one study reported on in the October 2002 edition of the Journal of Anesthesia and Analgesia proved that hot peppers, used as a topical treatment, could significantly reduce post-operative nausea and vomiting.

Turnips and Crushed Garlic

Therapeutic Uses: Invigorates the stomach to improve digestion. Clears away congestion. Fights viruses and helps to reduce blood pressure. Helps to purify blood and improve circulation. Treats chest congestion and excess phlegm. Helps to treat obesity.

Ingredients:

- 1 bulb of garlic (with purple peel)
- 1/2 pound of turnips
- 1/2 teaspoon of salt
- 1 tablespoon of soy sauce
- 1/2 tablespoon of vinegar
- 1 tablespoon of sesame oil

Directions:

1. Wash and shave turnip; then cut it into thin strips.
2. Combine turnips with salt, mix well and let stand for one day.
3. Crush garlic with a knife and remove the peel.
4. Drain off salt water from turnips.
5. Combine smashed garlic, soy sauce, vinegar, and sesame oil. Serve.

Serves 2.

Sweet Potato and Corn Congee

Therapeutic Uses: Warms the interior. Nourishes the stomach and spleen. Improves digestion. Helps recovery after illness.

Ingredients:

1/2 pound of sweet potato

1/2 cup of dried corn

8 cups of water

Directions:

1. Grind dried corn into coarse bits.
2. Peel sweet potatoes and cut into large cubes.
3. Put a pot with about 8 cups of water over high heat.
4. When water boils, reduce to low heat and add in corn to cook for 1 hour.
5. Add in sweet potato cubes and go on cooking for another half-hour, until cubes soften considerably. Serve.

Serves 2.

A TIP FROM THE MASTER

Because sweet potatoes and corn contain relatively high amounts of starch and sugar, people suffering from diabetes should avoid or limit this dish.

Tofu in Tomato Sauce

Therapeutic Uses: Invigorates the spleen. Stimulates appetite. Improves the production of body fluid to quench thirst. Helps digestion. Clears away heat. Facilitates the circulation of body fluid. Treats hypertension, obesity, high cholesterol, and poor appetite due to stomach deficiency.

Ingredients:

- 1/2 pound of tofu
- 1 cup of tomato sauce
- 1 teaspoon of salt
- 1 tablespoon of vinegar
- 1/2 tablespoon of raw sugar
- 1 tablespoon of green onions
- 1/2 tablespoon of ginger
- 2 tablespoons of vegetable oil
- 1/2 cup of water

Directions:

1. Cut tofu into half-inch cubes; then boil in water for 1 minute. Set aside.
2. Heat vegetable oil in wok over high heat. Slide in ginger and green onions and stir-fry for 15 seconds.
3. Add in tomato sauce and stir-fry for 30 seconds.
4. Pour in 1/2 cup of water.
5. Add in salt, vinegar, sugar and tofu cubes.
6. Cook until it boils. Serve.

Serves 2.

Tofu with Green Onions

Therapeutic Uses: Clears away heat inside the body. Nourishes the stomach. Stimulates poor appetite due to hot weather.

Directions:

1. Cut tofu into half-inch cubes.
2. Wash green onions and cut into small pieces.
3. Mix tofu, sesame oil, salt and green onion pieces together. Serve.

Ingredients:

1/2 pound of tofu

4 stalks of green onion

1/2 teaspoon of salt

1 tablespoon of sesame oil

Serves 2.

A TIP FROM THE MASTER

These days tofu is readily available in mainstream grocery stores. There are a number of kinds ranging from soft to firm. Experiment and choose the type that works best for you. You will probably find that different kinds work better for different recipes.

Simple Spiced-up Celery

Therapeutic Uses: Protects and clears blood vessels. Reduces blood pressure and protects blood capillaries. Treats hypertension, arteriosclerosis, obesity and diabetes.

Ingredients:

1 pound of fresh celery

1/2 teaspoon of salt

1 tablespoon of soy sauce

1 tablespoon of vinegar

1 tablespoon of sesame oil

8 cups of water

Directions:

1. Remove celery root and leaves. Wash and drain.
2. Put a wok with 8 cups of water over high heat until boiling.
3. Add in celery and cook for 6 minutes.
4. Transfer celery to a plate and let it cool down.
5. Cut celery into 1-inch pieces; then place in a large bowl.
6. Add salt, vinegar, soy sauce. and sesame to celery. Serve.

Serves 2.

A TIP FROM THE MASTER

This is not a good dish for people suffering with ulcers.

Sesame Spinach and Celery

Therapeutic Uses: Nourishes Ying. Clears away heat. Calms the liver. Reduces pressure and bloating. Improves urination. Lubricates intestines and helps to improve bowel movements. Treats hypertension with symptoms like headaches, dizziness, flushing, constipation, and restlessness. Helpful in treating diabetes.

Ingredients:

5 cups of fresh spinach

3 cups of celery

2 tablespoons of sesame oil

1/2 teaspoon of salt

Directions:

1. Remove celery leaves and roots. Wash spinach and celery.
2. Boil celery and spinach (separately) in water for 2 minutes each.
3. Remove celery and spinach and cut into 1-inch chunks.
4. Transfer vegetables to a plate.
5. Combine salt and sesame oil with celery and spinach. Serve.

Serves 2.

Hot Green Pepper With Bitter Melon

Therapeutic Uses: Clears away heat. Removes toxins. Lowers blood sugar. Treats diabetes, hypertension, and high cholesterol.

Ingredients:

- 3 small hot green peppers
- 1/2 pound of bitter melon
- 1 tablespoon of vinegar
- 1 tablespoon of soy sauce
- 1/2 teaspoon of salt
- 1 stalk of green onion
- 2 tablespoons of vegetable oil

Directions:

1. Cut green peppers into thin strips.
2. Cut the bitter melon in half and remove seeds; then slice into pieces.
3. Cut green onion into half-inch chunks.
4. Put pepper strips and bitter-melon pieces into a wok and dry-fry (no oil) for 3 minutes.
5. Pour vegetable oil into the wok; then slide in green onions, soy sauce, and salt. Stir-fry for 5 minutes.
6. Sprinkle on vinegar. Serve.

Serves 2.

A TIP FROM THE MASTER

Bitter melon can be purchased in many Asian and natural food stores.
A relative of the watermelon and squash, bitter melon resembles a bumpy cucumber.

Bitter Melon in Red-pepper Oil

Therapeutic Uses: Clears away heat in the body. Removes toxins. Lowers blood sugar. Treats diabetes, hypertension, obesity, and high cholesterol.

Directions:

1. Cut each bitter melon into two halves and remove seeds.
2. Cut diagonally into thin slices.
3. Put a wok with 4 cups of water over high heat. When it boils, put in bitter melon to boil 4 minutes. Remove to drain and let cool down.
4. Make sauce by mixing salt, soy sauce, sesame-oil, and green onion pieces.
5. Pour the sauce over the bitter melon. Serve.

Serves 2.

Ingredients:

1/2 pound of bitter melon

1 tablespoon of red-pepper oil

1/3 teaspoon of salt

1 tablespoon of soy sauce

2 tablespoons of sesame oil

1/2 tablespoon of green onion

4 cups of water

A TIP FROM THE MASTER

Bitter melon can be found in most Asian and natural food stores.

String Beans in Ginger Dressing

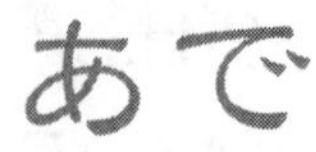

Therapeutic Uses: Warms the body. Lubricates the lungs to clear congestion. Treats cough. Removes toxins. Stimulates movement of the stomach to improve digestion. Strengthens the stomach. Suppresses vomiting. Helps to improve appetite. Clears away heat from the body. Treats hypertension and diabetes.

Ingredients:

1 pound of string beans

1 tablespoon of ginger pieces

1 tablespoon of vinegar

1 teaspoon of salt

3 tablespoons of sesame oil

8 cups of water

Directions:

1. Clean string beans.
2. Put about 8 cups of water in a wok over high heat until boiling.
3. Add in string beans and boil 10 minutes.
4. Transfer string beans to a bowl of cold water to cool. Once cooled, drain water from bowl.
5. Add salt to beans and let stand for 5 minutes. Drain off any excess water.
6. Chop ginger into thin pieces.
7. Make sauce by mixing ginger pieces, vinegar, and sesame oil.
8. Sprinkle the sauce over string beans.
9. Mix well and let the beans stand for 10 minutes. Serve.

Serves 3.

A TIP FROM THE MASTER

Ginger, which is naturally high in vitamin C, is often used to treat the symptoms of a cold.

Lotus Root With Green Onion

Therapeutic Uses: Invigorates the stomach and spleen. Nourishes blood. Treats chronic hepatitis and gastroduodenal ulcer.

Directions:

1. Shave lotus root and cut into thin slices.
2. Put 4 cups of water in a wok over high heat until boiling.
3. Add in lotus root slices and boil for 10 minutes.
4. Transfer lotus root slices to a bowl of cold water to cool. Drain and put on a plate.
5. Chop green onion into thin pieces.
6. Make sauce by mixing green onions and sesame oil.
7. Sprinkle the sauce over the lotus-root slices. Serve.

Serves 2.

Ingredients:

1 cup of lotus root

2 stalks of green onion

2 tablespoons of sesame oil

1/2 teaspoon of salt

4 cups of water

A TIP FROM THE MASTER

Lotus root can be found in most Asian grocery stores.

Lotus Root in Ginger Juice

Therapeutic Uses: Warms the body. Lubricates the lungs to relieve congestion. Treats coughs. Removes toxins. Stimulates the movement of the stomach to improve digestion. Strengthens the stomach and spleen. Suppresses vomiting. Treats stomach deficiency with symptoms like ache, indigestion, and bleeding.

Ingredients:

1 tablespoon of ginger bits

1 cup of lotus root

3 tablespoons of sesame oil

1 tablespoon of soy sauce

1/2 teaspoon of salt

2 teaspoons of vinegar

4 cups of water

Directions:

1. Shave lotus root and cut into thin slices.
2. Put 4 cups of water in a wok over high heat until boiling.
3. Add in lotus root slices and boil for 10 minutes. Remove and set aside.
4. Shave the ginger; then slice and chop it into bits.
5. Make sauce by mixing ginger, soy sauce, salt, sesame-oil, and vinegar.
6. Pour the sauce over the lotus root slices and serve.

Serves 2.

A TIP FROM THE MASTER

Lotus root can be found in most Asian grocery stores.

Green Bell Pepper with Green Bean Sprouts

あで

Therapeutic Uses: Clears away heat. Facilitates circulation of body fluid. Treats hypertension and diabetes, especially in the summer.

Directions:

1. Wash bean sprouts and pepper.
2. Cut green pepper into thick strips.
3. Heat vegetable oil in wok over high heat. Slide in pepper strips and stir-fry for 3 minutes.
4. Slide in green bean sprouts.
5. Add in salt and continue stir-frying for another 2 minutes. Serve.

Serves 2.

Ingredients:

1/2 pound of green bean sprouts

1 green bell pepper

1 teaspoon of salt

2 tablespoons of vegetable oil

A TIP FROM THE MASTER

Green bean sprouts, also known as mung bean sprouts, can be purchased in most Asian food stores, natural food stores, and many mainstream grocery stores.

Green Bean Sprouts With Chives

Therapeutic Uses: Reinvigorates the kidney. Purges pathogenic heat and toxins. Treats hypertension, diabetes, and fatigue in the loins and knees due to kidney deficiency. Helps treat obesity.

Ingredients:

- 1/2 pound of green bean sprouts
- 1/2 cup of chives
- 1 teaspoon of salt
- 1 tablespoon of vegetable oil

Directions:

1. Wash green bean sprouts and drain.
2. Wash chives and cut into 1-inch strips.
3. Heat vegetable oil in wok over high heat. Slide in green bean sprouts and chives together.
4. Stir-fry for 4 minutes.
5. Add in salt and mix well. Serve.

Serves 2.

A TIP FROM THE MASTER

Green bean sprouts, also known as mung bean sprouts, can be purchased in most Asian and natural food stores. You can also grow your own using a sprouter.

Sweet and Sour Yellow Bean Sprouts あの

Therapeutic Uses: Rich source of plant protein. Helps to treat hypertension, cardiovascular diseases, edema and constipation.

Directions:

1. Wash bean sprouts and drain.
2. Boil bean sprouts in water for 1 minute. Remove and drain.
3. Make sauce by combining salt, green onions, vinegar, sesame-oil, and sugar.
4. Sprinkle sauce over the bean sprouts. Serve.

Serves 1.

Ingredients:

- 1/3 pound of yellow bean sprouts
- 3 teaspoons of raw sugar
- 2 teaspoons of vinegar
- 1 teaspoon of salt
- 2 tablespoons of sesame oil
- 1 tablespoon of green onion pieces

A TIP FROM THE MASTER

Yellow bean sprouts are sprouted from soybeans. They are larger and more distinctive in flavor than green bean (mung bean) sprouts and can be found in most Asian food stores.

Simmered Celery, Kelp, and Carrot

Therapeutic Uses: Clears heat away from the kidneys. Facilitates blood circulation. Calms the liver. Clears congestion. Reduces blood pressure. Lowers cholesterol. Acts as a cancer preventive. Helps treat obesity.

Ingredients:

3 stalks of celery

1/2 cup of kelp

3 carrots

2 tablespoons of vegetable oil

1 teaspoon of soy sauce

2 tablespoons of cooking wine

1 teaspoon of salt

stalk of fennel

1 tablespoon of scallion

Directions:

1. Soak kelp in cold water for 1 hour.
2. Wash kelp and soak it again in warm water for a half-hour.
3. Cut kelp in large pieces and transfer to a small soup pot.
4. Add enough cold water to immerse the kelp.
5. Simmer over medium heat for a half-hour.
6. Add 1 tablespoon of cooking wine, 1 teaspoon of soy sauce and fennel. Reduce to low heat and simmer another half-hour.
7. Remove and let cool; then cut kelp into strips and let stand.
8. Remove roots and leaves from celery; then wash and shake off water.
9. Cut into half-inch stems and let stand.

Simmered Celery, Kelp, and Carrot, continued

10. Wash carrots and cut into thin slices.
11. Heat wok over high heat; then slide in carrots and dry-fry (no oil) for 8 minutes. Remove and let stand.
12. Heat vegetable oil over medium heat and cook celery for 5 minutes.
13. Slide in carrots; then add remaining cooking wine and 1 teaspoon of salt and stir-fry for another 3 minutes.
14. Slide in kelp strips and add 2 tablespoons of water.
15. Simmer for 5 minutes.
16. Sprinkle on scallion pieces. Serve.

Serves 1.

A TIP FROM THE MASTER

Kelp is a nutrition packed sea vegetable often used in Chinese dishes. It can be purchased in most Asian food stores.

Steamed Eggplant

Therapeutic Uses: Removes toxins from blood. Eliminates edema. Stops bleeding. Induces diuresis. Enhances the functions of blood capillaries. Helps to treat hypertension.

Ingredients:

2 eggplants

1/2 teaspoon of salt

2 tablespoons of soy sauce

1/8 cup of sesame-oil

1 stalk of green onion

Directions:

1. Wash the eggplants; then cut each into four large pieces and put them into a large bowl.
2. Put the bowl on a steaming rack into a pot with water. Fill with water to 1 inch before water surface touches the bowl.
3. Steam for 25 minutes and then remove the bowl.
4. While the eggplant is hot, sprinkle on salt, soy sauce, sesame oil and scallion pieces. Serve.

Serves 2.

String Beans, Tomato, and Tofu

Therapeutic Uses: Treats hypertension, diabetes, and chronic fatigue.

Directions:

1. Boil string beans in water for 1 minute. Drain and let stand.
2. Cut tofu into 1-inch pieces.
3. Boil tofu in water for 1 minute. Drain and let stand.
4. Cut tomato into small sections.
5. Soak dried shrimp in warm water for half an hour. Drain and let stand.
6. Heat vegetable oil in the wok over high heat; then stir-fry scallions and ginger pieces for 10 seconds.
7. Slide in tomato pieces and stir-fry for 1 minute.
8. Add 4 tablespoons of water, slide in tofu, soaked shrimp, and string beans. Stir-fry for 5 minutes.
9. Add salt and remove from heat. Serve.

Serves 2.

Ingredients:

1/2 pound of fresh tofu

2 tomatoes

1 cup of string beans

1 tablespoon of ginger

2 tablespoons of scallions

1 tablespoon of vegetable oil

1/2 tablespoon of starch

2 tablespoons of dried shrimp

1 teaspoon of salt

4 tablespoons of water

A TIP FROM THE MASTER

Tofu can be found in mainstream grocery stores, Asian, food markets, and natural food stores.

Yellow Bean Sprout Sauté あの

Therapeutic Uses: Nourishes the spleen and stomach. Clears blood vessels. Removes swellings. Nourishes the large intestines. Reduces cholesterol. Treats cardiovascular disease, hypertension, edema, and constipation.

Ingredients:

- 1/2 pound of yellow bean sprouts
- 2 tablespoons of vegetable oil
- 1 teaspoon of salt
- 1/2 tablespoon of soy sauce
- 1 tablespoon of cooking wine
- 1/2 tablespoon of green onion pieces
- 1/2 cup of water

Directions:

1. Remove roots from sprouts. Wash and drain.
2. Heat vegetable oil over high heat; then slide in bean sprouts and stir-fry for 5 minutes.
3. Add salt, cooking wine, and soy sauce; then stir-fry for another 3 minutes.
4. Add a half cup of water, cover the wok and simmer for 6 minutes.
5. Sprinkle in green onion pieces and continue stir-frying for another 2 minutes.
6. Remove from heat. Serve.

Serves 3.

A TIP FROM THE MASTER

Yellow bean sprouts, grown from soybeans, can be purchased in many Asian food stores and natural food stores.

Peanuts and Celery

Therapeutic Uses: Restores blood vessels. Lowers blood pressure. Reduces gas and bloating. Improves vision. Calms the mind. Induces diuresis.

Directions:

1. Heat cooking oil in a pan for 1 minute.
2. Add peanuts, fry until crispy and move to a plate.
3. Cut celery into 1-inch slices.
4. Boil celery in water for 30 seconds; then remove and rinse in cold water. Drain off any excess water.
5. Arrange the celery around the plate and place peanuts at the center.
6. Put soy sauce, salt, sugar, vinegar, and pepper oil into a small bowl and mix well.
7. Pour the mixture into the dish. Serve.

Serves 1.

Ingredients:

1/3 cup of peanuts
3 stalks of celery
1/2 teaspoon of salt
1 tablespoon of soy sauce
1/2 tablespoon of sugar
1/2 tablespoon of vinegar
1 tablespoon of cooking oil
1/4 tablespoon of pepper oil

A TIP FROM THE MASTER

Peanuts, which have been around for 3,500 years, are actually not nuts at all. They are members of the legume family.

White-bean and Snow Peas Sauté

Therapeutic Uses: Clears away heat. Restores blood circulation. Helps improve appetite. Helps to treat hypertension.

Ingredients:

- 1/2 pound of dried white bean curd
- 1 cup of snow peas
- 1 red pepper
- 1 tablespoon of vegetable oil
- 1/2 tablespoon of soy sauce
- 1/2 tablespoon of raw sugar
- 1 teaspoon of salt
- 1 teaspoon of ginger
- 1 tablespoon of onions
- 1/2 tablespoon of starch
- 2 tablespoons of water

Directions:

1. Cut red peppers into small strips and dried white bean curd into half-inch cubes.
2. Put dried bean curd into boiling water. Put snow peas into a separate pot of boiling water. Allow both to boil for a brief time and drain.
3. Put cooking oil into a wok and heat for about 1 minute. Add onions and ginger.
4. Add bean curd and fry for 1 minute.
5. Add red pepper, snow peas, soy sauce, sugar, salt and 2 tablespoons of water.
6. Dissolve starch with a little bit of water and add to the mixture. Mix evenly. Serve.

Serves 2.

A TIP FROM THE MASTER

White bean curd, made of pressed soybeans, resembles a soft cheese and can be purchased in most Asian food stores as well as online.

Stir-fried Mushrooms With Celery

Therapeutic Uses: Clears away heat. Calms the liver. Replenishes qi and blood. Treats hypertension and diabetes.

Ingredients:

- 1/2 pound of celery
- 10 water soaked mushrooms
- 1 tablespoon of vegetable oil
- 1/2 teaspoon of salt
- 1/2 tablespoon of vinegar
- 1/2 tablespoon of soy sauce
- 1 tablespoon of starch
- 4 tablespoons of water

Directions:

1. Cut celery into 1-inch strips.
2. Mix celery with salt and let stand for about 10 minutes. Rinse and drain.
3. Cut mushrooms into pieces.
4. Put starch, vinegar, and 4 tablespoons of water into a bowl to make a thin paste. Set aside.
5. Stir-fry the celery in hot oil for 2 or 3 minutes; then put in mushroom pieces and stir-fry quickly.
6. Add soy sauce and stir for 1 minute.
7. Add in paste and mix well. Serve.

Serves 2.

A TIP FROM THE MASTER

The first records of the farming of mushrooms date back to 7th century China.

Hot and Sour Potato Strips

Therapeutic Uses: Stimulates poor appetite caused by stomach or intestinal disorders.

Ingredients:

1/2 pound of potatoes

2 tablespoons of vinegar

3 pieces of red chili

1 teaspoon of salt

2 tablespoons of vegetable oil

Directions:

1. Peel potatoes and cut into thin pieces.
2. Rinse with cold water to remove starch on the surface, drain and transfer potato pieces to a plate.
3. Cut red chili into thin strips.
4. Heat vegetable oil in wok over high heat; then slide in chili and stir-fry for 5 seconds.
5. Slide in potato strips and stir-fry for 8 minutes, until potatoes are tender.
6. Sprinkle with vinegar and mix well. Serve.

Serves 2.

A TIP FROM THE MASTER

An easy rule of thumb to follow when trying to figure out the proper dropping order of the ingredients when stir frying is that thicker firmer vegetables and meats like carrots and beef will need to cook longer than more tender and less dense ingredients such as mushrooms or sprouts.

Hot Green Pepper With Potato Strips あの

Therapeutic Uses: Stimulates appetite. Reinvigorates the stomach. Treats loin pain due to weak stomach, fatigue and constipation. Helps to treat hypertension and heart disease.

Directions:

1. Wash hot green peppers and potatoes.
2. Cut peppers and potatoes into small strips.
3. Rinse potato strips to remove starch on the surface. Drain and let stand.
4. Heat vegetable oil in wok over high heat; then slide in peppers and stir-fry until you can smell their fragrance. Remove peppers and discard.
5. Add in potato strips and pepper and stir-fry for 8 minutes, until potatoes are tender.
6. Add salt and mix well. Serve.

Serves 4.

Ingredients:

10 hot green peppers

1 pound of potatoes

1 teaspoon of salt

1/2 tablespoon of pepper

3 tablespoons of vegetable oil

Celery, Hot Pepper, and Potato Strips

あで

Therapeutic Uses: Strengthens the stomach. Treats stomachache, chronic constipation, vomiting, ulcers, hypertension, and diabetes.

Ingredients:

1 pound of potatoes

1/2 pound of celery

2 fresh red hot peppers or 1 red bell pepper

2 tablespoons of vegetable oil

1 tablespoon of soy sauce

1 tablespoon of sesame oil

1/2 tablespoon of vinegar

1/2 teaspoon of salt

1 stalk of green onion

1/2 tablespoon of raw sugar

Directions:

1. Peel the potatoes and cut into small pieces. Do the same with red peppers and green onion.
2. Remove celery leaves and roots. Cut into 1-inch slices.
3. Drop the potatoes into boiling water for half a minute. Cool down with cold water. Drain and let them stand.
4. Make sauce by mixing salt, sugar, vinegar, sesame oil, and soy sauce.
5. Heat vegetable oil in wok over high heat. Fry green onion strips quickly and then add in potatoes, celery and red pepper. Stir-fry for 10 minutes, until potatoes are tender.
6. Sprinkle in mixed sauce. Fry for 1 more minute. Serve.

Serves 4.

Bamboo Shoots With Green Onions 

Therapeutic Uses: Facilitates circulation of blood and other body fluids. Quenches thirst due to excess heat in the body. Treats hypertension and diabetes.

Ingredients:

1/2 pound of bamboo shoots

3 stalks of green onion

1/2 teaspoon of salt

2 tablespoons of sesame oil

4 tablespoons of hot water

Directions:

1. Wash bamboo shoots and cut into small strips.
2. Boil in water for 3 minutes; then remove, drain and let stand on a plate.
3. Wash green onions and cut into thin strips.
4. Make sauce by mixing salt, sesame oil, and 4 tablespoons of hot water.
5. Sprinkle the sauce over bamboo shoots. Serve.

Serves 2.

A TIP FROM THE MASTER

Over 4,000 species of bamboo are grown in China. In fact, China produces the most bamboo of any country in the world.

Hot Green Peppers With Bamboo Shoots

あで

Therapeutic Uses: Facilitates circulation of blood and other body fluids. Quenches thirst due to excess heat inside the body. Treats hypertension and diabetes.

Ingredients:

3 hot green peppers

1/2 pound of bamboo shoots

1/2 teaspoon of salt

2 tablespoons of sesame oil

1 tablespoon of vegetable oil

Directions:

1. Wash peppers and cut into rings.
2. Cut bamboo shoots into small strips.
3. Boil pepper rings and bamboo shoot strips in water for 3 minutes; then drain and let stand on a plate.
4. Heat vegetable oil and sesame oil in wok over high heat.
5. Pour the heated oil over the pepper pieces and bamboo shoot strips on the plate.
6. Add salt and mix well. Serve.

Serves 2.

A TIP FROM THE MASTER

Bamboo is an important part of Chinese culture having been used for everything from paper to food to household items. The importance of bamboo, a symbol for integrity in China, can be seen reflected in the works of many Chinese artists.

Spicy Bite Radishes

Therapeutic Uses: Clears heat. Nourishes blood. Facilitates the circulation of body fluid. Treats hypertension, constipation, and swelling. Acts as a cancer preventive.

Directions:

1. Wash radishes and cut into thin strips.
2. Add salt to radishes and allow to stand for 10 minutes. Drain off the saltwater.
3. Make sauce by mixing red-chili oil, soy sauce, sesame oil, and sugar.
4. Sprinkle the sauce over the radish strips. Serve.

Serves 2.

Ingredients:

1/2 pound of red radishes

2 teaspoons of soy sauce

2 teaspoons of red chili oil

2 tablespoons of sesame oil

1/2 teaspoon of salt

1 teaspoon of raw sugar

A TIP FROM THE MASTER

Spicy hot red chili oil is a common ingredient in Chinese cooking. You can purchase a prepared sauce from an Asian food store, the international aisle at your local mainstream grocery store, or online. If you prefer to make your own sauce at home you will need 1/2 cup of peanut or canola oil, 20 dried red chili peppers, 1/8 teaspoon of ground cumin, and a dash of salt. Heat the oil in a small sauce pan over a medium to high heat until hot. Add the peppers and reduce to a low heat cooking uncovered and stirring occasionally until the peppers turn a dark brown color. Remove oil from heat, add in cumin and salt, and mix well. Use a strainer lined with paper towels or a coffee filter to remove the solids. Transfer the strained oil to a clean airtight jar and keep in the refrigerator for up to six months.

Chinese Broccoli Sauté

Therapeutic Uses: Clears away heat. Facilitates the circulation of body fluid. Nourishes stomach and intestines. Treats indigestion, obesity, and thirst due to overheating in the stomach and spleen.

Ingredients:

1 pound of Chinese broccoli

2 teaspoons of garlic bits

2 tablespoons of vegetable oil

1/2 teaspoon of salt

Directions:

1. Wash Chinese broccoli and drain.
2. Heat vegetable oil over high heat; then slide in garlic and stir-fry for 10 seconds.
3. Slide in Chinese broccoli and stir-fry for 5 minutes.
4. Add in salt and mix well. Serve.

Serves 4.

A TIP FROM THE MASTER

The flowering stems of Chinese broccoli are sold in bunches in Asian grocery stores and natural food stores. Chinese brocolli, sometimes called Chinese kale, is a member of the mustard family and has a slightly bitey or peppery taste followed by a lightly bitter aftertaste.

Asparagus Lettuce Strips in Sesame Paste

Therapeutic Uses: Facilitates the production of body fluid. Purges heat in the body. Treats hypertension, diabetes, indigestion, and osteoporosis.

Ingredients:

1 pound of asparagus lettuce

2 tablespoons of sesame oil

2 tablespoons of sesame paste

1/2 teaspoon of salt

1/2 tablespoon of raw sugar

1/2 cup of warm water

Directions:

1. Cut lettuce into thin strips.
2. Boil lettuce strips in water for 1 minute; then drain and let stand on a plate.
3. Combine sesame paste with 1/2 cup of warm water; then add salt, sugar and sesame oil.
4. Pour the sauce over the lettuce strips. Serve.

Serves 4.

A TIP FROM THE MASTER

Asparagus lettuce, which looks like a cross between celery and lettuce, can be found in almost any Asian grocery store as well as some mainstream and natural foods stores.

Succulent Asparagus-lettuce Strips

Therapeutic Uses: Nourishes the stomach and spleen. Stimulates appetite. Facilitates the production of body fluid. Clears away heat. Treats hypertension and diabetes. Excellent dish for people on a diet or for those suffering from obesity.

Ingredients:

- 1 pound of asparagus lettuce
- 3 teaspoons of coriander chips
- 1 teaspoon of green onions
- 1/2 tablespoon of pepper
- 1 teaspoon of raw sugar
- 1 tablespoon of sesame paste
- 3 teaspoons of soy sauce
- 1 teaspoon of vinegar
- 2 teaspoons of red-chili oil
- 1/2 teaspoon of salt
- 2 tablespoons of sesame oil
- 1/2 tablespoon of garlic

Directions:

1. Shave the lettuce and cut into thin strips.
2. Combine the strips with salt and a cup of warm water and soak for 5 minutes.
3. Make sauce by mixing sesame paste, soy sauce, vinegar, sesame oil, pepper, sugar, garlic and coriander.
4. Pour the sauce over the lettuce strips. Serve.

Serves 4.

A TIP FROM THE MASTER

Asparagus lettuce, which resembles a cross between celery and lettuce, can be found in most Asian grocery stores as well as some mainstream and natural foods stores.

Carrot Sautéed in Butter

Therapeutic Uses: Invigorates the lungs. Acts as a stomach and spleen tonic. Dries dampness and removes congestion. Provides heat to defend against cold. Treats stomach and spleen deficiencies.

Directions:

1. Shave carrot and cut into thin strips.
2. Boil strips in water for 5 to 6 minutes (being careful not to make them too tender), drain and let stand.
3. Cut onion into strips.
4. Heat butter in wok over medium heat; slide in onion strips and stir-fry for 5 minutes, until they turn brown.
5. Slide in carrot strips and add salt, pepper and a half-cup of water.
6. Cover the wok and simmer over medium heat for 5 minutes. Serve.

Serves 2.

Ingredients:

1/2 pound of carrots

2 tablespoons of cooking wine

1/2 teaspoon of salt

1/2 tablespoon of pepper

1/5 cup of onions

2 tablespoons of butter

1/2 cup of water

Hot Green Pepper With Eggplant

Therapeutic Uses: Protects blood vessels. Facilitates circulation of body fluids. Treats cardiovascular diseases and swelling.

Ingredients:

3 hot green peppers

1/2 pound of eggplant

4 tablespoons of vegetable oil

1 tablespoon of soy sauce

1/3 teaspoon of salt

1/3 teaspoon of pepper

1 tablespoon of green onions

1 tablespoon of garlic

Directions:

1. Clean the hot green peppers and remove seeds.
2. Cut peppers into match-size strips.
3. Wash the eggplant and cut into match-size strips.
4. Heat vegetable oil in wok over high heat, slide in green onions and pepper. Stir-fry for 10 seconds.
5. Slide in eggplant strips to stir-fry for 5 minutes.
6. Slide in hot green pepper and continue to stir-fry for another 3 minutes.
7. Add soy sauce and salt and stir-fry for 1 minute. Serve.

Serves 2.

Eggplant with Potatoes あの

Therapeutic Uses: Helps with stomach weakness. Improves the functions of stomach and intestines. Protects blood vessels. Treats chronic fatigue, constipation and cardiovascular diseases.

Directions:

1. Wash eggplant and potatoes.
2. Place in a bowl and steam over boiling water for 30 minutes.
3. Remove their peels and smash the potatoes and eggplant into a paste.
4. Combine eggplant and potato paste with half the salt and mix well.
5. Boil eggs; then remove the shells and separate the yolks from the whites.
6. Smash the yolks into a paste and chop the whites into thin pieces.
7. Divide remaining salt and add 1/2 to the yolk paste and sprinkle other 1/2 over egg white pieces.
8. Put eggplant and potato paste in the center of a plate and yolk paste and white pieces beside it.
9. Sprinkle on sesame oil and coriander. Mix and serve.

Serves 4.

Ingredients:

1 pound of eggplant

1 pound of potatoes

3 eggs

3 tablespoons of coriander

2 teaspoons of salt

1 tablespoon of sesame oil

A TIP FROM THE MASTER

For all you hummus lovers out there this dish is a good alternative choice and a delicious change of pace. The general consistency of the dish is like that of hummus and the eggs add in that all-important protein.

Savory Eggplant Strip Sauté

Therapeutic Uses: Protects blood vessels. Facilitates the circulation of body fluids. Treats cardiovascular disease, hypertension, diabetes, obesity and swelling.

Ingredients:

- 1/2 pound of eggplant
- 4 tablespoons of vegetable oil
- 2 tablespoons of soy sauce
- 1/2 teaspoon of salt
- 1/2 teaspoon of pepper
- 1/2 tablespoon of garlic
- 1/2 tablespoon of green onions

Directions:

1. Clean eggplant and cut into match-size strips.
2. Soak eggplant strips in cold water for 3 minutes and remove to drain.
3. Heat vegetable oil in wok over high heat; then slide in pepper, garlic and green onions. Stir-fry for 10 seconds.
4. Slide in eggplant strips and stir-fry for 8 minutes.
5. Add in soy sauce and salt; then stir-fry for 1 more minute. Serve.

Serves 2.

A TIP FROM THE MASTER

In China a dye was made from eggplant and used to stain the teeth of ladies of the court.

Mixed Vegetable Omelet

Therapeutic Uses: Replenishes protein in the body. Replenishes vital energy. Treats chronic fatigue due to kidney and stomach deficiencies.

Directions:

1. Wash and cut squash, onions and green onions into small pieces.
2. Cut hot green peppers into thin slices.
3. Beat and whip eggs.
4. Mix egg with squash, green onions and onions.
5. Combine with olive, oil, pepper and hot green pepper pieces. Mix well.
6. Put a pan over medium heat; then pour in egg mixture to completely cover pan bottom.
7. When egg mixture is set, loosen edges and flip egg to cook other side. When both sides are set, remove to serve.

Serves 1.

Ingredients:

2 eggs

1/2 pound of squash

3 tablespoons of onion

2 stalks of green onion

2 hot green peppers

2 tablespoons of olive oil

1/2 tablespoon of pepper

Bitter Melon with Soybeans Omelet  

Therapeutic Uses: Reduces blood pressure. Calms the gall bladder. Treats asthma, cancer, and wakefulness.

Ingredients:

1 pound of bitter melon

1/2 cup of soybeans

1 tablespoon of soy sauce

1 tablespoon of sesame oil

1 teaspoon of vinegar

4 eggs

2 tablespoons olive oil

Directions:

1. Cut each bitter melon in half, remove seeds and chop into slices.
2. Boil bitter melon in water for 2 minutes; then remove and set aside.
3. Put soybeans in boiling water to cook for 15 minutes.
4. Remove soybeans and set aside.
5. Heat oil in wok and add in eggs, bitter melon slices, and soybeans and stir fry until the eggs set.
6. Place omelet on a plate and sprinkle on soy sauce, sesame oil and vinegar. Serve.

Serves 4.

A TIP FROM THE MASTER

Bitter melon resembles a cucumber in general color, shape, and size. However, the skin of this cucumber-relative is very bumpy in comparison. Bitter melon and soybeans can be found in most Asian food stores.

Cauliflower in Stewed Sauce

Therapeutic Uses: Serves as an ideal food for preventing cancer. Replenishes needed vitamins in the body. Treats cancer, hypertension, and diabetes.

Directions:

1. Break off cauliflower into small chunks.
2. Cut carrot into slices.
3. Soak dried mushrooms for 1 hour.
4. Boil carrot and soaked mushrooms for 1 minute. Remove, drain and let stand.
5. Heat vegetable oil in wok over high heat; then slide in chopped green onion followed by cauliflower, carrots and mushrooms. Stir-fry for 3 minutes.
6. Add in cooking wine, salt, sugar, soy sauce and 5 tablespoons of water. Cook until fluid in wok boils.
7. Dissolve cornstarch in water then add. Sprinkle on pepper oil. Serve.

Serves 4.

Ingredients:

1 pound of cauliflower

3 small carrots

5 dried mushrooms

2 tablespoons of vegetable oil

2 tablespoon of soy sauce

1 tablespoon of cooking wine

1/2 teaspoon of raw sugar

1/2 teaspoon of salt

1/2 tablespoon of pepper oil

1/2 tablespoon of cornstarch

1/2 tablespoon of green onion

5 tablespoons of water

Simple Sesame Tofu Dip

Therapeutic Uses: Lubricates intestines. Provides rich plant protein. Serves as an ideal food for people suffering from hypertension or diabetes and for people on diet.

Ingredients:

1/2 pound of tofu

2 tablespoons of soy sauce

1 tablespoon of sesame oil

Directions:

1. Cut tofu into 1-inch cubes.
2. Mix soy sauce and sesame oil.
3. Dip tofu cubes into the mixture of soy sauce and sesame oil before eating.

Serves 2.

A TIP FROM THE MASTER

Tofu is a soft cheese-like product made from soymilk. It is very high in protein and because of its bland flavor and spongy consistency it is a chameleon that picks up the taste of whatever you are cooking it with or whatever sauce you are dipping it into. There are both soft and hard varieties of tofu and which kind you use is generally a matter of taste as well as the type of dish you intend to add it to. A firmer tofu will probably work better for dipping purposes while a soft tofu might be preferred in certain soups. Experiment and find what type works best for you.

Tofu Strips with Garlic

Therapeutic Uses: Facilitates the production of body fluid. Provides protein needed by the human body. Helps to clean the stomach and intestines. Is an ideal food for people suffering from hypertension or diabetes, and for people on a diet.

Directions:

1. Crush garlic and chop it into thin pieces.
2. Mix garlic chips, soy sauce, and vinegar.
3. Sprinkle the mixture over tofu cubes. Serve.

Serves 2.

Ingredients:

1/2 pound of tofu cubed

3 cloves of garlic

2 tablespoons of soy sauce

1 tablespoon of vinegar

A TIP FROM THE MASTER

Tofu is widely available in mainstream grocery stores and Asian markets. Tofu choices range from soft through firm. A firmer tofu will probably work better for dipping purposes.

Shredded Green Bell Pepper and Eggplant あの

Therapeutic Uses: Helps to purify blood to relieve swelling and pain. High in Vitamin P, which can enhance cells' adhesion and improves the resistance of small blood vessels to viruses. Treats blood vessel diseases like hypertension, hemoptysis, and arteriosclerosis.

Ingredients:

1 green bell pepper

1 eggplant

2 tablespoons of vegetable oil

1 teaspoon of soy sauce

1/2 teaspoon of salt

1/2 tablespoon of corn-starch

1/2 tablespoon of green onions

1/2 tablespoon of garlic

Directions:

1. Wash and cut green bell pepper and eggplant into match-size strips.
2. Heat oil in wok over high heat; then slide in green onions, followed by eggplant strips and stir-fry for 3 minutes.
3. Slide in pepper strips and continue frying for another 5 minutes.
4. Add soy sauce and salt, followed by cornstarch dissolved in 3 tablespoons of water.
5. Add in garlic and mix well. Serve.

Serves 2.

Spinach Sauté

Therapeutic Uses: Facilitates blood circulation. Cleans the stomach and intestines. Adjusts vital energy. Stops restlessness. Quenches thirst. Lubricates the lungs.

Directions:

1. Wash the spinach (keeping red roots) and drain.
2. Heat oil in wok over high heat and add in spinach.
3. Stir-fry for 1 minute.
4. Add soy sauce, sugar, and salt. Mix well. Serve.

Serves 2.

Ingredients:

1/2 pound of fresh spinach

2 tablespoons of vegetable oil

1 tablespoon of soy sauce

1/2 teaspoon of salt

1/2 tablespoon of raw sugar

Spinach With Sesame

Therapeutic Uses: Serves as an ideal food for hypertension, diabetes and people on a diet.

Ingredients:

1/2 pound of spinach

1 1/2 tablespoons of sesame oil

2 tablespoons of soy sauce

1/2 teaspoon of salt

1 clove of garlic

1 teaspoon of vinegar

Directions:

1. Wash spinach and cut into 2-inch strips.
2. Crush garlic and chop into thin pieces.
3. Put spinach strips into boiling water; then cook for two minutes, remove and drain.
4. Sprinkle sesame oil, soy sauce, vinegar, and garlic over the spinach. Mix and serve.

Serves 2.

A TIP FROM THE MASTER

Garlic has been used medicinally for at least 3,000 years.

Sweet and Sour Kelp

Therapeutic Uses: Nourishes the blood and qi. Clears congestion and other obstructions. Softens blood vessels. Clears away excessive heat from the body. Helps to lower blood cholesterol. Prevents fat accumulation. Treats arteriosclerosis, hypertension, swollen glands and edema.

Directions:

1. Cut kelp into 3-inch strips and put into a large bowl.
2. Add soy sauce, vinegar, sugar and salt. Mix well.
3. Add hot sauce to taste.
4. Add sesame oil, mix well. Serve.

Serves 2.

Ingredients:

- 3 cups of soaked kelp
- 1 tablespoon of soy sauce
- 1 tablespoon of vinegar
- 1/2 tablespoon of raw sugar
- 1/2 teaspoon of salt
- 1 tablespoon of sesame oil
- 1 tablespoon of hot sauce (optional)

A TIP FROM THE MASTER

Kelp is a common sea vegetable often used in Asian cooking. This nutritionally dense vegetable is packed with calcium, potassium, chromium, magnesium, iodine, copper, zinc and iron. Kelp can be purchased in most Asian grocery stores.

To fully tenderize dried kelp soak it for about one hour in warm water. Alternately, to speed the process, you may simmer the kelp in water for 15 to 20 minutes or pressure-cook it for about five minutes.

Sautéed String Beans

Therapeutic Uses: Helps provide a balanced nutrition. Treats hypertension, chronic fatigue and diabetes.

Ingredients:

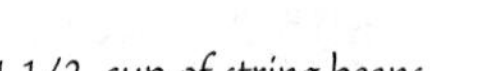

- 1 1/2 cup of string beans
- 2 tablespoons of vegetable oil
- 1/2 teaspoon of salt
- 2 teaspoons of soy sauce
- 1 tablespoon of green onions
- 1/2 tablespoon of garlic
- 5 tablespoons of water

Directions:

1. Wash and break string beans into 1-inch strips.
2. Heat vegetable oil in wok over high heat; then slide in green onions and stir-fry for 10 seconds.
3. Slide in string beans and stir-fry for 5 minutes.
4. Add in soy sauce, salt and 5 tablespoons of water. Cover the wok, reduce to low heat and simmer for 10 minutes.
5. Add in garlic and turn up to high heat. Continue stir-frying for 2 minutes. Serve.

Serves 1.

Fried Eggplant あの

Therapeutic Uses: Protects blood vessels. Treats blood vessel diseases like hypertension, hemoptysis, and arteriosclerosis.

Directions:

1. Wash and peel eggplant; then cut into half-inch slices.
2. Heat vegetable oil in wok over high heat; then slide in eggplant and deep-fry until golden. Remove eggplant from wok, drain off oil, and let stand.
3. Make sauce by mixing soy sauce, ginger, green onions, and cornstarch with 1 cup of warm water.
4. Remove all but two tablespoons of oil from wok and turn on high heat.
5. Add in garlic and stir-fry for 10 seconds.
6. Put mixed sauce and eggplant into wok. Stir-fry for 2 minutes. Serve.

Serves 2.

Ingredients:

2 small eggplants

2 tablespoons of soy sauce

1/2 teaspoon of salt

2 cups of vegetable oil

1 tablespoon of cornstarch

1/2 tablespoon of ginger strips

1 tablespoon of green onions

1/2 teaspoon of garlic

1 cup of warm water

Wok Fried Turnips

Therapeutic Uses: Helps to maintain a balanced metabolism. Improves appetite. Improves digestion, especially of greasy food. Soothes qi. Eliminates congestion. Relieves asthma. Helps to regulate urination. Quenches thirst. Treats indigestion, an inflated belly, cough with congestion, chest congestion, and the flu.

Ingredients:

2 cups of turnips

2 teaspoons of soy sauce

1/2 teaspoon of salt

2 tablespoons vegetable oil

2 tablespoons of cornstarch

1/2 tablespoon of ginger strips

1 tablespoon of green onions

1/2 teaspoon of garlic

Directions:

1. Wash and slice turnips into thick strips.
2. Heat 1 tablespoon of oil in wok over high heat; then slide in turnip strips and stir-fry for 3 minutes. Remove from wok and let stand.
3. In a soup bowl make the sauce by mixing soy sauce, salt, starch, ginger strips, green onions and garlic bits. Fill bowl halfway with water and mix.
4. Heat remaining 1 tablespoon of oil over high heat. Put in mixed sauce and turnip strips at the same time and stir-fry for 3 minutes. Serve.

Serves 2.

A TIP FROM THE MASTER

Why not try taking a few moments before you eat to prepare to eat? Take time to notice and be thankful for the variety of foods you are about to eat. And take a moment to make sure that you are truly hungry and not just eating out of habit or boredom.

White-gourd Sauté

Therapeutic Uses: Helps the circulation of body fluid to improve urination. Nourishes the liver. Purges excessive body heat. Harmonizes the stomach to adjust vital energy. Treats hypertension, obesity, constipation, and liver disease.

Ingredients:

- 1 1/2 pounds of white gourd
- 2 tablespoons of soy sauce
- 1/2 teaspoon of salt
- 4 tablespoons of vegetable oil
- 2 tablespoons of cornstarch

Directions:

1. Peel white gourd and cut into 1-inch cubes.
2. Dissolve starch in 1/2 cup of water.
3. Put white gourd cubes in boiling water for 3 minutes, until they look transparent. Remove, drain and let cool.
4. Heat vegetable oil in wok over high heat; then add in soy sauce, salt, and 2 cups of water.
5. When the sauce boils, slide in white-gourd cubes, and reduce to low heat. Simmer for 5 minutes.
6. Increase to high heat. Add cornstarch dissolved in water and stir for 30 seconds to make sauce thicker. Serve.

Serves 4.

A TIP FROM THE MASTER

The white gourd (also called wax gourd, winter melon, Cassababa, and Chinese preserving melon) is a round to oblong shaped gourd found in most Asian markets as well as many fresh foods and natural foods markets.

Healing Rice and Noodle Dishes

Rice and noodles are an integral part of Chinese and other Asian cuisines. Both filling and satisfying rice and noodles are the perfect base for building a variety of healthy and hearty meals.

Steamed Rice

Ingredients:

1 cup of white rice

3 cups of water

Directions:

1. Put rice in a heatproof bowl.
2. Pour 1 1/2 cups of water into the bowl. Put a rack in a pressure cooker.
3. Pour 1 1/2 cups of water in cooker. Carefully lower the bowl onto the rack inside the pressure cooker and ensure that there is enough room around and above the bowl.
4. Close the lid. **For safety purposes please check the hole (vent pipe) of the lid BEFORE using. Make sure that it is completely unclogged.**
5. Put the pressure pot on your stove.
6. Set to high heat until you can hear the water boiling (or pressure is reached); Turn down heat to medium.
7. Allow rice to cook for about 5 minutes.
8. Turn off the heat, remove the pot and let the pressure drop gradually by itself before opening lid; Very carefully remove lid and bowl. Serve.

Serves 2.

A TIP FROM THE MASTER

A pressure cooker is called for in this recipe because it cooks rice quickly. However rice can also be cooked in a saucepan with a tightly fitting lid according to package directions. Whenever using a pressure cooker please always use extra caution to avoid being scalded or burned.

Boiled Rice

Directions:

1. For the regular pot method, put the desired amount of rice in a pot and add water until the water surface is 1 inch above the rice. For the pressure cooker, put 5 cups of water in cooker and bring to a boil before adding 2 cups of rice.
2. Cover the pot. **When using a pressure cooker, be sure to check the lid's vent hole to make sure it is completely unclogged BEFORE covering the pot with it.**
3. For a regular pot, keep the heat at medium temperature until no water is above the rice, switch heat to low.
4. For pressure pot, set the heat to maximum and when the pressure is reached, turn heat down to medium and cook for 5 minutes.
5. Rotate the pot so that each section gets cooked evenly.
6. Remove pot from heat. Keep regular pot covered for at least one minute. For pressure cooker, let the cooker cool by itself for about 8 minutes, then press the finger-tip control lightly to release pressure. Serve.

Serves 2.

Ingredients:

Rice

Water

A TIP FROM THE MASTER

To the Chinese, rice is seen as a symbol for life itself. Many common Chinese phrases such as the greeting "Have you had your rice today?" attest to the importance of rice to the culture. Although the exact origins of the grain are not know most experts can agree that rice most likely got its start in India and was probably first cultivated as a crop in southeast Asia.

White Rice Congee

Therapeutic Uses: Treats a weak stomach and heart disease. Ideal dish for those on a diet.

Ingredients:

1 cup white rice

7 1/2 cups of water

Directions:

1. Rinse rice lightly.
2. Put 1 cup of rice and 7 1/2 cups of water in a regular pot (or pressure cooker).
3. Put partially covered pot on the range top. **When using a pressure cooker check the lid's vent hole to make sure it is unclogged BEFORE covering the pot.**
4. For the regular pot, keep heat at medium temperature for about 5 minutes, then switch heat to low and simmer for 1 hour. Stir occasionally.
5. For the pressure pot, set the heat to maximum and when the vent nozzle stops spraying, turn the heat down to medium and simmer for 20 minutes.
6. Rotate the pot so that each section gets cooked evenly.
7. Remove pot from heat. Keep regular pot covered for at least one minute. Let pressure cooker cool down for 5 to 8 minutes, then press the finger-tip control to release pressure. Remove lid. Serve.

Serves 2.

A TIP FROM THE MASTER

The Chinese were the first to cultivate rice in water in fields known as rice paddies. The rice seeds, which begin their life cycle in a dry bed, are transferred about a month or so later into a rice paddie to complete the growing process.

Fortune Fried Rice

Therapeutic Uses: Balances nutrition. Replenishes protein in the body. Relieves constipation. Lubricates the intestines. Helps to treat diabetes.

Directions:

1. Cut mushrooms, cooked pork, and bamboo shoots into 1/4-inch cubes.
2. Beat the egg in a bowl; then add 1/2 teaspoon of salt. Mix well.
3. Heat 1 tablespoon of olive oil over medium heat, slide in egg mixture and cook for 30 seconds. Transfer to a bowl.
4. Heat remaining olive oil over high heat. Slide in mushrooms, pork, bamboo shoots, snow peas and carrot slices. Stir-fry for 5 minutes.
5. Add in cooking wine, the remaining 1/2 teaspoon of salt, and half a cup of water.
6. Continue stir-frying for 3 minutes.
7. Add in white rice and egg and stir-fry for 6 minutes.
8. Sprinkle on green onion pieces and stir several times. Serve

Serves 2.

Ingredients:

3 cups of cooked white rice

1/3 pound of lean cooked pork

1/4 pound of bamboo shoots

2/3 cup of snow peas

2/3 cup of thinly sliced carrots

3 soaked dried mushrooms

2 eggs

2 tablespoons of cooking wine

1 teaspoon of salt (divided in half)

4 tablespoons of olive oil

1 tablespoon of green onion pieces

1/2 cup of water

Scallop Fried Rice

Therapeutic Uses: Replenishes protein and vitamins in the body. Nourishes the kidneys and brain. Improves vision. Treats hypertension, diabetes and obesity.

Ingredients:

3 cups of cooked white rice

1/3 pound of scallops

1/4 pound of Asparagus lettuce

2 eggs

1 teaspoon of salt

1/2 teaspoon of pepper

2 tablespoons of olive oil

2 teaspoons of soy sauce

Directions:

1. Cut scallops and Asparagus lettuce into half-inch pieces.
2. Hard boil eggs. Remove their shells and cut them into 6 pieces.
3. Heat oil in wok over high heat. Add in cooked white rice and stir-fry for 3 minutes until hot.
4. Slide in scallops, Asparagus lettuce, and eggs and stir-fry for 5 minutes.
5. Add in salt, pepper and soy sauce. Go on stir-frying for another 2 minutes. Serve.

Serves 2.

A TIP FROM THE MASTER

Asparagus lettuce looks something like a cross between celery and lettuce and has a deliciously mild taste resembling a combination of a summer squash and an artichoke. You can find the lettuce in many Asian grocery stores as well as some mainstream and natural food stores.

Vegetable Rice Casserole

Therapeutic Uses: Is good for lubricating intestines. Improves the digestion. Helps to treat hypertension, diabetes, obesity, cancer and high cholesterol.

Ingredients:

- 1 1/2 cups of white rice
- 1/2 cup of onions
- 2 tablespoons of vegetable oil
- 3 soaked dried mushrooms (soak until tender)
- 2/3 cup of snow peas
- 2/3 cup of carrot slices
- 1/2 teaspoon of salt
- 2 teaspoons of soy sauce
- 1 small green pepper

Directions:

1. Wash white rice and drain.
2. Wash green pepper and boil in water. Remove pepper and cut into small pieces.
3. Cut onions, carrots and soaked mushroom into small pieces.
4. Heat vegetable oil over medium heat. Slide in onion and carrot pieces and stir-fry for 3 minutes.
5. Add white rice; Add in water until the water level is about 1/2 inch above the level of the rice. Cover wok to boil for 20 minutes.
6. Remove the cover; then add mushrooms, green pepper, snow peas and soy sauce.
7. Mix well and reduce to low heat to cook for another 5 minutes. Serve.

Serves 3.

A TIP FROM THE MASTER

Onions can cause gas and bloating in some people. If you are sensitive to onion you can omit it from this dish. You can substitute celery, white gourd, or the stems of asparagus lettuce for the onion if you wish.

Stewed Lamb Rice あので

Therapeutic Uses: Good dish to serve in the summer. Helps to treat hypertension, heart disease, and diabetes.

Ingredients:

- 1 pound of leg of lamb
- 3 cups of white rice
- 2 cloves of garlic
- 3 stalks of green onions (white part only)
- 1 cup of snow peas
- 2/3 cup of celery
- 1/2 teaspoon of ginger strips
- 5 pieces of dried red pepper
- 4 teaspoons of cooking wine
- 2 teaspoons of salt
- 2 teaspoons of soy sauce
- 1 teaspoon of pepper
- 2 tablespoons of peanut oil

Directions:

1. Cut lamb meat into 1-inch cubes and put in a bowl.
2. Rub lamb with 1 teaspoon of salt and 1 teaspoon of pepper and allow to stand for 1/2 hour.
3. Cut green onion, celery, ginger, garlic, and red pepper into small pieces.
4. Heat peanut-oil over high heat, slide in the lamb cubes and deep-fry until they turn golden.
5. Remove lamb and drain off excess oil.
6. Leave half of the oil in the wok. Add in ginger, green onions, celery, dried red peppers and lamb.
7. Add 2 cups of water and bring to a boil.
8. Add cooking wine, the remaining salt, and 2 teaspoons soy sauce.
9. Reduce heat to low and cook 10 minutes.
10. Add in white rice and snow peas. Mix well.
11. Pour in just enough water to immerse the mixture.
12. Reduce heat to low and stew for about 25 minutes, until rice is cooked.
13. Remove from heat. Serve.

Serves 4.

Tasty Cold Noodles

Therapeutic Uses: Clears away excessive heat from the body. Nourishes the stomach and spleen. Replenishes protein in the body. Treats poor appetite and indigestion.

Directions:

1. Boil noodles until tender. Drain, set aside, and allow to cool.
2. Boil bean sprouts in water for 1 minute. Remove and drain.
3. Dry-fry sesame seeds in a pan until done; then grind seeds into a powder while still hot.
4. Make sauce by combining green onions, ginger juice, garlic, sesame powder, soy sauce, vinegar, sesame paste and hot sauce in a bowl and mixing well.
5. Put bean sprouts over the noodles and sprinkle on the mixed sauce.
6. Sprinkle on sesame-oil. Serve.

Serves 2.

Ingredients:

1/2 pound of Chinese noodles

1 cup of bean sprouts

1 tablespoon of green onions

1/2 tablespoon of ginger juice

2 tablespoons of soy sauce

1/2 tablespoon of vinegar

1 tablespoon of sesame paste

1/2 teaspoon of hot sauce

1 tablespoon of sesame oil

2 teaspoons of sesame seeds

1/2 teaspoon of garlic

A TIP FROM THE MASTER

You can purchase prepared ginger juice from an Asian grocery store or online. You can also make your own ginger juice in a juicer or garlic press. Fresh squeezed ginger juice will remain fresh for about a week covered in the refrigerator. Chinese noodles are available in any Asian food market and many mainstream grocery stores as well.

Pork Chow Mein

Therapeutic Uses: Nourishes intestines. Protects blood vessels. Cleans the intestines. Treats arteriosclerosis and indigestion.

Ingredients:

1/2 pound of Chinese noodles

1/3 pound of lean pork

1/4 pound of spinach

2 tablespoons of vegetable oil

1/8 cup of green onions

1 teaspoon of salt

Directions:

1. Cut pork into 2-inch-thick strips.
2. Wash spinach and cut into 1-inch strips.
3. Cook noodles in boiling water until tender. Remove and drain.
4. Heat 1 tablespoon of vegetable oil in wok over medium heat; then slide in pork strips and stir-fry for 3 minutes. Remove pork.
5. Add remaining oil to wok and add in noodles to stir-fry for 4 minutes.
6. Combine salt, pork strips, green-onions, and spinach and stir-fry for another 3 minutes.
7. Remove from heat and serve.

Serves 2.

A TIP FROM THE MASTER

The noodle is a symbol of long life in China and as a result Chinese noodles are most often served long and uncut. You can find Chinese noodles in an Asian food store and many mainstream grocery stores as well.

Chicken Chow Mein あの

Therapeutic Uses: Replenishes proteins and vitamins in the body. Restores energy. Treats hypertension and high cholesterol.

Directions:

1. Cut chicken into thin strips.
2. Cut ginger and green onions into half-inch strips.
3. Remove egg yolks and whip egg whites.
4. Put chicken strips in a bowl, combine 1 teaspoon of salt, egg whites and cornstarch. Mix well and let stand.
5. Heat olive oil in wok over medium heat; then slide in chicken strips and deep-fry until they turn white. Transfer and drain.
6. Leave about 2 tablespoons of olive oil in wok; then slide in ginger and green onion strips and stir-fry for 3 minutes.
7. Add in bean sprouts and stir-fry for 3 minutes.
8. Put in remaining salt and chicken broth. Bring to a boil. Transfer to a large bowl.
9. Cook noodles until done. Drain and transfer to a plate to let cool down.
10. Put 1 tablespoon olive oil in wok; add the noodles when oil gets hot.
11. Stir-fry until noodles turn golden on both sides.
12. Pour in broth mixture, cover wok and simmer for 5 minutes.
13. Add in chicken strips and mix well. Serve.

Serves 2.

Ingredients:

1/2 pound of Chinese noodles

1/3 pound of chicken white meat

2 eggs

2/3 cup of bean sprouts

2/3 cup of olive oil

1 teaspoon of ginger strips

1/3 cup of green onions

2 teaspoons of salt

1/2 tablespoon of cornstarch

1 cups of chicken (or pork) broth

Steamed Spinach Noodles

Therapeutic Uses: Nourishes intestines. Protects blood vessels. Cleans the intestines. Treats arteriosclerosis, hypertension, cancer, and indigestion.

Ingredients:

1 pound of Chinese noodles

1/2 pound of spinach

1 tablespoon of sesame oil

1 teaspoon of salt

1 cup of chicken (or pork) broth

Directions:

1. Cook noodles until done. Transfer and let stand.
2. Wash spinach and cut into 2-inch strips.
3. Combine chicken broth and salt in a bowl. Mix well.
4. Add in noodles and spinach strips.
5. Put the bowl in a steamer (or a large pot with water) to steam for 10 minutes.
6. Remove the bowl, add soy sauce to taste, and sprinkle with sesame-oil to serve.

Serves 4.

A TIP FROM THE MASTER

The noodle has been a staple of the Chinese diet since the Han dynasty over 5,000 years ago. Chinese noodles are available in any Asian market as well as many mainstream grocery stores.

Noodles Topped with Tomato and Pork

Therapeutic Uses: Facilitates the circulation of body fluid. Improves urine flow. Relieves swelling. Helps to treat hyperplasia of the prostate.

Ingredients:

- 1/2 pound of Chinese noodles
- 1/3 pound of pork
- 2 medium tomatoes
- 2 tablespoons of olive oil
- 1 teaspoon of green onions
- 1 teaspoon of ginger strips
- 1 teaspoon of salt
- 3 cups of chicken (or pork) broth

Directions:

1. Cut pork into thin strips.
2. Boil tomatoes in water until peels become soft. Remove peels and cut tomatoes into thick pieces.
3. Cut ginger and green onion into thin strips.
4. Heat olive oil in wok, then slide in pork strips, ginger and green onion strips and stir-fry for 3 minutes.
5. Pour in chicken broth and cook until boiling.
6. Add noodles into the wok and cook for 9 minutes.
7. Put in tomato pieces and add salt. Mix evenly.
8. When it boils again, remove from heat. Serve.

Serves 2.

A TIP FROM THE MASTER

Chinese noodles are available in any Asian market as well as many mainstream grocery stores.

Healing Desserts

Although the Chinese generally don't eat desserts in the Western sense of the word these sweet treats are sure to please whether you are satisfying your own sweet tooth or fixing them for a crowd.

Banana With Juice

Therapeutic Uses: Calms the liver. Removes excessive heat from the body. Helps to treat headache, dizziness, and tinnitus caused by hypertension. Improves quality of sleep.

Ingredients:

3 bananas

2/3 cup of corn

1/2 cup of watermelon peel (rind)

1/3 cup of raw sugar

1/2 cup of hawthorn berries

2 cups of water

Directions:

1. Peel bananas and cut into thick pieces.
2. Combine banana pieces with 2 tablespoons of raw sugar in a bowl.
3. Cover the bowl with a piece of wet etamine or cheesecloth and steam for half an hour.
4. Cut watermelon peel into small pieces.
5. Pour 2 cups of water into a pot. Add watermelon peels, corn and hawthorn and cook in the pot over high heat for 20 minutes.
6. Takes 1 cup of mixed juice from the pot and filter it through the etamine or cheesecloth.
7. Stir remaining raw sugar into the mixed juice and pour the mixture over the steamed banana in the bowl. Serve.

Serves 3.

A TIP FROM THE MASTER

The peels or rinds of a number of fruits and melons are commonly used in the creation of tasty treats in China. Although this practice might seem a bit strange at first glance, give it a try. This process is very much like using the bones from a chicken or shells from shrimp to create a soup stock. Try next time you are craving something sweet and I am sure you will be pleasantly surprised.

Watermelon Congee

Therapeutic Uses: Removes summer heat. Calms the mind. Stimulates urination. Reduces swelling due to kidney disorders, diabetes, and choleplania. Ideal dish in the summer for people working in high-temperature environments.

Directions:

1. Wash watermelon peels and rice.
2. Put rice into a pot and pour in 8 cups of water. Heat over medium heat until it boils.
3. Reduce to a low heat and stew for another 45 minutes.
4. Put in watermelon peels and simmer for another 15 minutes.
5. Remove and discard watermelon peels.
6. Add in raw sugar and mix well. Serve.

Serves 2.

Ingredients:

1 cup of watermelon peels

1 cup of white rice

2 tablespoons of raw sugar

8 cups of water

A TIP FROM THE MASTER

It is not uncommon in China to use the nutrition packed rind of a fruit or vegetable to help in the creation of a dish. It is a more simplified and pure way of living when we learn to utilize all that we have and reduce the wastefulness in our lives.

Lotus Leaf Congee

Therapeutic Uses: Clears excessive heat from the body. Invigorates yang of the spleen. Dissolves stasis to stop bleeding. Used to treat sunstroke and dizziness in the summer. Treats hypertension, high blood fat, and obesity.

Ingredients:

1 piece of fresh lotus leaf

1 cup of rice

1 tablespoon of raw sugar

8 cups of water

Directions:

1. Wash lotus leaf and rice.
2. Cut lotus leaf into 4 large pieces.
3. Put rice into a pot, pour in 8 cups of water and keep on medium heat until it boils.
4. Reduce to low heat and stew for another 50 minutes.
5. Stir in lotus leave pieces and go on simmering for another 15 minutes.
6. Remove and discard leaves.
7. Add raw sugar and mix well. Serve.

Serves 2.

A TIP FROM THE MASTER

The lotus first appeared in Chinese literature and poetry about 3,000 years ago. It has come to symbolize spiritual renewal and female beauty. The lotus is felt to have a number of healing properties. You can find fresh lotus leaf in an Asian grocery store.

Pear Congee

Therapeutic Uses: Clears away excessive heat to stop a cough. Stimulates the production of body fluid to quench thirst. Protects the throat. Serves as an ideal food for singers, broadcasters and teachers.

Directions:

1. Wash pears and rice.
2. Peel pear and cut it into small chunks (discard core).
3. Put rice and 5 cups of water in a pot and bring to a boil over medium heat.
4. Add in pear. Reduce to a low heat and simmer for 1 hour, until fluid becomes very thick.
5. Add in raw sugar and stir until it melts. Serve.

Serves 1.

Ingredients:

1 pear

1/2 cup of rice

5 cups of water

1 tablespoon of raw sugar

Tremella (White-tree-fungi) Soup

Therapeutic Uses: Nourishes yin and the stomach. Produces body fluid Regulates the blood. Used to beautify the skin. Especially good as supplement food for patients with a sustained low fever.

Ingredients:

1 cup of tremella

2 tablespoons of raw sugar

5 cups of water

Directions:

1. Wash the tremella in warm water to remove any dirt.
2. Soak it in 5 cups of cold water for one day. The tremella will become swollen and transparent.
3. Pour the tremella together with the soaking water into a steel pot.
4. Add raw sugar
5. Simmer over low heat for at least 1 hour until the tremella turns soft. Serve.

Serves 1.

A TIP FROM THE MASTER

Tremella is a type of fungus, like mushrooms, that can be found in most Asian grocery stores or herb shops. It should be a pure creamy white color and when dried will still retain a clean and fresh appearance. A sure sign that tremella is getting old is when you notice it starting to crumble.

Date and Lotus Seed Soup あの

Therapeutic Uses: Enhances the heart. Invigorates the spleen. Calms the mind. Stabilizes blood pressure and stimulates blood circulation. Improves heart functions. Improves appetite. Helps improve quality of sleep.

Directions:

1. Soak dates in warm water for about 5 minutes. Wash and drain.
2. Soak lotus seeds in hot water until they swell and soften.
3. Put the lotus seeds in a steel pot, add 10 cups of water and bring to a boil over high heat.
4. Once boiling, reduce heat to low and simmer for 1 hour.
5. Add dates and sugar to stew for another 30 minutes (or until lotus seeds and dates turn soft). Serve.

Serves 3.

Ingredients:

10 dates

1 cup of lotus seeds

1 tablespoon of raw sugar

10 cups of water

A TIP FROM THE MASTER

Lotus seeds can be purchased in most Asian grocery stores as well as through online sources.

This dish can be served over white rice if desired.

Lotus Seed Pudding

Therapeutic Uses: Nourishes the kidneys. Invigorates the spleen. Nourishes the heart. Calms the mind. Helps combat fatigue. Stimulates a poor appetite. Relieves loin pain in men due to excessive seminal emission Treats excessive discharge for women. Serves as an ideal food for office workers and young couples. Acts as a cancer preventive.

Ingredients:

1/2 cup of white lotus seeds

1/10 ounce of ginseng

5 red dates

2 tablespoons of raw sugar

8 cups of water

Directions:

1. Wash lotus seeds with cold water and red dates with warm water.
2. Put lotus seeds, ginseng and red dates in a bowl. Pour in 8 cups of water.
3. Cover the bowl and put it into a pot with water. Use a steamer rack if available.
4. Put the pot on low heat to steam for 2 hours.
5. Add raw sugar to the bowl. Cover and steam for another hour, until the lotus seeds become very tender.
6. Carefully remove bowl. Serve.

Serves 2.

A TIP FROM THE MASTER

Red dates, which are high in vitamin C, are often served at celebrations to symbolize hope for prosperity. Both red dates and lotus seeds can be purchased in Asian grocery stores as well as through online sources.

Papaya and Coix-seed Soup

Therapeutic Uses: Nourishes the liver. Relaxes stiff and sore muscles. Alleviates water retention and swelling. Regulates the stomach. Relieves abdominal distension. Effective in treating ankle and knee-joint pains.

Directions:

1. Put clean papaya pieces and coix seeds into a steel pot and 7 cups of water.
2. Soak for 10 minutes.
3. Put the pot over low heat and simmer until coix seeds begin to melt.
4. Add raw sugar and simmer for another 10 minutes. Serve.

Serves 2.

Ingredients:

1/3 pound of papaya

1/5 pound of coix seed

1 tablespoon of raw sugar

7 cups of water

A TIP FROM THE MASTER

Coix seeds, often called Job's Tears in the United States, are a cereal grain grown in central and southern Asia. You can purchase the seeds in most Asian grocery stores and many natural food stores.

Lotus Seed Congee

Therapeutic Uses: Invigorates the kidney. Nourishes the heart. Cleans the intestines. Treats loose bowels caused by a spleen deficiency. Reduces excessive seminal emission due to kidney deficiency. Reduces frequent urination at night. Treats night sweats.

Ingredients:

1/2 cup of lotus seeds

1 cup of sticky rice

3 tablespoons of brown sugar

8 cups of water

Directions:

1. Wash lotus seeds and crush them into large pieces.
2. Wash sticky rice.
3. Put sticky rice and lotus seeds in a pot. Pour in 8 cups of water.
4. Put the pot on medium heat and cook until it boils.
5. Reduce heat to low and simmer for 1 hour until the soup becomes thick.
6. Add in brown sugar. Mix well. Serve.

Serves 3.

A TIP FROM THE MASTER

Lotus seeds can be purchased in most Asian grocery stores.

Chinese Yam with Black Sesame Seeds

Therapeutic Uses: Invigorates the spleen and stomach. Nourishes the lungs and kidneys. Relieves fatigue. Treats poor appetite due to hypofunction of the spleen. Helps relieve cough and asthma due to lung deficiency. Is used to treat problematic seminal emission and frequent urination due to kidney deficiency.

Directions:

1. Wash black sesame seeds. Dry-fry 10 minutes, until you can smell the fragrance.
2. Peel Chinese yam and cut into half-inch thick pieces.
3. Heat vegetable oil in wok over medium. Slide in yam and deep-fry until they float (they will be crisp on the surface and tender inside).
4. Transfer yam pieces to a plate and let stand.
5. Remove oil from wok and replace with sugar and a cup of water. Stir-fry quickly until the sugar melts.
6. Push in yam pieces and stir continuously until they are coated completely with sugar.
7. Remove yam pieces. Sprinkle on black sesame seeds. Serve.

Serves 1.

Ingredients:

- 1 Chinese yam
- 1 tablespoon of black sesame seeds
- 1 tablespoon of raw sugar
- 3 tablespoons of vegetable oil
- 1 cup of water

A TIP FROM THE MASTER

Black sesame seeds are stronger in aroma and flavor than white sesame seeds. They can be purchased in most Asian and Indian grocery stores. Chinese yams, or shan yao, can be found in most Asian grocery stores. If you are unable to find Chinese yams you may substitute a common yam.

Chinese-yam Congee

Therapeutic Uses: Strengthens the spleen. Nourishes the stomach and kidneys. Invigorates the lungs. Stimulates appetite. Treats loose bowels caused by deficiencies of the spleen and the stomach. Helps malnourished children. Treats abnormal female discharge. Reduces cough caused by deficiency in the lung. Treats trouble with seminal emission and enuresis due to deficiency in the kidney. Helps treat for chronic gastritis.

Ingredients:

2 fresh Chinese yams

1 cup of sticky rice

2 tablespoons of raw sugar

8 cups of water

Directions:

1. Peel the yams and cut into 1-inch cubes.
2. Wash sticky rice.
3. Put yam cubes and sticky rice in a pot and pour in 8 cups of water. Cook over medium heat until boiling.
4. Reduce to low heat and simmer for 1 hour, until the fluid inside the pot becomes very thick. Stir occasionally.
5. Add in raw sugar and mix well. Serve.

Serves 2.

A TIP FROM THE MASTER

Chinese yams can be found in most Asian grocery stores. If you are unable to find Chinese yams you may substitute common yams.

Tremella Congee

Therapeutic Uses: Restores yin. Lubricates the lungs. Facilitates the production of body fluid. Nourishes the stomach. Treats cough, blood in the phlegm and constipation.

Directions:

1. Soak tremella in hot water until it swells.
2. Clean fungus carefully to remove dirt.
3. Clean rice and red dates.
4. Put white fungus, rice, and dates in a pot. Pour in 9 cups of water.
5. Put the pot over medium heat until it boils.
6. Reduce to low heat and cook for about 1 hour, until fluid in the pot becomes very thick.
7. Add in raw sugar and simmer for another 5 minutes. Serve.

Serves 2.

Ingredients:

1 cup of tremella (white fungus)

1 cup of rice

5 red dates

1 1/2 tablespoons of raw sugar

9 cups of water

A TIP FROM THE MASTER

Like mushrooms, tremella is a type of fungus. It can be found in most Asian grocery stores or herb shops. It should be a pure creamy white color and when dried will still retain a clean and fresh appearance. A sure sign that tremella is getting too old is when you notice it starting to crumble.

Honey Walnut Kernel

Therapeutic Uses: Nourishes the kidney to reduce seminal emission. Calms asthma and cough due to deficiency in the kidney. Counteracts constipation due to intestinal dryness. Treats seniors suffering from bronchitis or constipation.

Ingredients:

1 cup of fresh walnut kernels

1/3 cup of honey

1 tablespoon of raw sugar

5 red cherries

1 tangerine

Directions:

1. Soak the walnut kernels in boiling water and remove any excess skin. Put them in a bowl.
2. Add raw sugar and put the bowl in a pot with water to steam for 15 minutes.
3. Put steamed walnut kernels on a plate (reserving the juice that resulted from steaming separately). Place tangerine sections and cherries over the kernels.
4. Put a pan over low heat and add in honey. Cook until boiling. Pour in the kernel juice and mix well.
5. Pour the mixture of honey and kernel juice over the walnut kernels. Serve.

Serves 2.

Lotus Root Congee

Therapeutic Uses: Invigorates the spleen. Stimulates appetite. Replenishes the blood. Treats diarrhea. Helps to treat fatigue, poor appetite, and loose bowels due to underfunctioning of the spleen and stomach. Relieves thirst during convalescence.

Directions:

1. Shave the lotus root's surface.
2. Cut the lotus root into half-inch slices.
3. Wash sticky rice.
4. Put lotus root slices and sticky rice together in a soup pot. Pour in 8 cups of water.
5. Cook over medium heat until boiling. Reduce heat to low and simmer for about 1 hour, until the fluid becomes very thick.
6. Add brown sugar and mix well. Serve.

Serves 2.

Ingredients:

1/2 cup of fresh lotus root

1 cup of sticky rice

2 tablespoons of brown sugar

8 cups of water

A TIP FROM THE MASTER

Fresh lotus root can be purchased in most Asian grocery stores. The root is reminiscent of water chestnuts in taste and texture. Canned lotus root is also available in stores and online and is an acceptable alternative if fresh roots cannot be found. But of course fresh is always best.

Wolfberry Fruit Congee

Therapeutic Uses: Nourishes the kidneys. Replenishes the blood. Nourishes yin. Improves vision. Can treat weakness in the loins and knees. Treats dizziness. Fights deficiencies of the liver and kidney.

Ingredients:

1/2 cup of Wolfberry fruits

1/2 cup of rice

1 1/2 tablespoons of raw sugar

5 cups of water

Directions:

1. Wash wolfberry fruit and rice. Put them in a soup pot and pour in 5 cups of water. Cook over medium heat till boiling.

3. Reduce to low heat and simmer for 1 hour, until the fluid becomes very thick.

4. Add in sugar and mix well. Serve.

Serves 1.

A TIP FROM THE MASTER

Wolfberry fruit, or gou qi zi in Chinese, are the bright-red sweet berries of a woody shrub that is native to China and Tibet. The Wolfberry fruit, also known as Lycium, can be found in some Asian grocery stores, health food stores, or natural food stores. The berries are not widely available yet in this country, but with some persistence you probably can track down a resource. To make an alternate, but similar, dessert you may substitute raisins or prunes in this recipe.

APPENDIX I

Individual Food Nutrition & Healing Properties

As much as I would like to I can't be there personally to advise you on your specific food choices so I have done the next best thing. I designed this section for you to use as a quick-reference tool. I have laid the section out alphabetically so you can easily locate an individual food and see, at a glance, information about that foods taste, nature, and important nutritional highlights.

The food items are divided into categories under which I list the specific taste and nature of the food (for example warm, cold, sweet, and hot), the general nutritional content, and then, perhaps most importantly, the overall therapeutic character of each food. You can look up the main ingredients in any dish you wish to prepare and get a good idea of the overall balance and properties of that dish. Use this section as a guide to creating your own balanced healthy meals.

MEAT

Beef : *sweet, warm*

Nutritional Highlights :

Protein, fat, sodium, phosphorus, potassium, selenium, niacin, and vitamins B-6, B-12, and E

Therapeutic Actions :

Replenishes vital energy, strengthens the spleen, nourishes the stomach, strengthens bones and muscles, and promotes the circulation of body fluids to relieve swelling

Lamb : *sweet, hot*

Nutritional Highlights :

Protein, fat, sodium, niacin, potassium, manganese, calcium, iron, and vitamins A, B-6, E, and C

Therapeutic Actions :

Fights fatigue, treats lung disease, and treats anemia

Pork : *sweet and salty, neutral*

Nutritional Highlights :

Protein, fat, phosphorus, potassium, selenium, and vitamins A and E

Therapeutic Actions :

Nourishes blood vessels and lubricates muscles and skin

POULTRY

Chicken : *sweet and salty, neutral*

Nutritional Highlights :

Protein, fat, phosphorus, sodium, selenium, magnesium, potassium, and vitamins A and E

Therapeutic Actions :

Refreshes the five organs, nourishes the spleen and stomach, strengthens muscles and bones, promotes blood circulation, and regulates menstruation

Duck : *sweet and salty, slightly cold*

Nutritional Highlights :

Protein, fat, potassium, phosphorus, zinc, selenium, retinal, and vitamins A and E

Therapeutic Actions :

Nourishes yin, restores deficiencies, alleviates cough, promotes circulation of body fluids, and resolves phlegm

DAIRY

Eggs : *neutral, sweet*

Nutritional Highlights :

Protein, calcium, phosphorus, potassium, sodium, selenium, folate, retinal, and vitamins A, B-6, B-12, and E

Therapeutic Actions :

Replenishes blood, relieves dryness, reinvigorates vital energy, and relieves fatigue

Note : *Eggs are particularly good for women after giving birth. Those with elevated cholesterol levels should avoid egg yolks, which are high in cholesterol.*

Milk : *sweet, neutral to slightly warm*

Nutritional Highlights :

Protein, lactose, fat, calcium, potassium, phosphorus, vitamins A, B-6, B-12, C, and D

Therapeutic Actions :

Nourishes blood, restores vital energy, combats fatigue, nourishes skin and hair, moisturizes the lungs, and improves vision

SEAFOOD

Carp : *sweet, warm*

Nutritional Highlights :

Protein, fat, sodium, phosphorus, potassium, selenium, niacin, and vitamins A, E and B

Therapeutic Actions :

Warms the body and promotes the circulation of body fluid to relieve swelling

Ocean Crab : *salty, cold*

Nutritional Highlights :

Protein, fat, calcium, phosphorus, potassium, sodium, selenium, iron, retinol and vitamins A, B-12 and B-6

Therapeutic Actions :

Acts as a liver and stomach tonic, activates blood, cools internal heat sensations, and facilitates recovery of dislocations

Note : *Because of ocean crab's cold nature it should be avoided if you suffer from stomach deficiencies. Those suffering with gout should avoid crab because it is very high in protein.*

Crucian : *sweet, neutral*

Nutritional Highlights :

Protein, fat, calcium, iron, phosphorus, potassium, selenium, niacin, retinol, and vitamins A and B

Therapeutic Actions :

Promotes the production of body fluid (especially milk production after giving birth) and strengthens the stomach

Eel : *sweet, neutral*

Nutritional Highlights :

Protein, fat, calcium, phosphorus, potassium, sodium, retinal, vitamin A and B-12

Therapeutic Actions :

Treats lung disease

Shrimp (fresh and dried) : *sweet, warm*

Nutritional Highlights :

Protein, fat, phosphorus, iron, potassium, sodium, selenium, vitamins A and D

Therapeutic Actions :

Invigorates the kidney to enhance yang, treats impotence, fights fatigue, treats weaknesses in the loins and knees, promotes milk production, and clears away toxins such as the ones that lead to cellulitis and ulcers

Note : *Those suffering with gout should avoid shrimp because it is high in protein*

Soft Shell Turtle : *salty, neutral*

Nutritional Elements :

Protein, fat, sugar, niacin, mineral salt, and vitamins B-1 and B-2

Therapeutic Actions :

Nourishes yin, suppresses yang, resolves stasis of body fluids, useful for treating prolapse of the uterus

Note : *You should avoid eating too much soft shell crab because it can be damaging to the stomach. If you normally suffer from a poor appetite or indigestion you should avoid soft shell crab.*

VEGETABLES

Alfalfa Sprouts : *cool, bitter*

Nutritional Elements :

Phosphorus, potassium, calcium, manganese, copper, folate, vitamin A

Therapeutic Actions :

Acts as a tonic for the stomach and spleen, expels dampness from the body, and lubricates the intestines

Asparagus : *sweet and bitter, cool*

Nutritional Elements :

Calcium, potassium, folate, fiber, and vitamins A, E, C and B-6

Therapeutic Actions :

Clears heat from the body, expels dampness, and relieves water retention

Bamboo Shoots : *sweet, cold*

Nutritional Elements :

Potassium, phosphorus, calcium, fiber, and vitamins A, C, B-6, and E

Therapeutic Actions :

Clears interior heat, detoxifies the body, balances the warm energy of meat, treats cardiovascular diseases, diabetes, and obesity

Bitter melon : *bitter, cold*

Nutritional Elements :

Calcium, sodium, niacin, and vitamins E and C

Therapeutic Actions :

Fights diabetes, improves glucose tolerance, and treats the symptoms of HIV

Carrot : *sweet, slightly warm*

Nutritional Elements :

Carotene, sugar, potassium, sodium, calcium, manganese, vitamins A, C, and E

Therapeutic Actions :

Reinvigorates the stomach, improves digestion, dispels worms, improves vision, lowers blood pressure, and accelerates the discharge of mercury from body

Celery : *sweet, cold*

Nutritional Elements :

Calcium, magnesium, phosphorus, potassium, sodium, and vitamins A, B-6, C, and E

Therapeutic Actions :

Cleanses the stomach, removes heat, cleans and protects blood vessels, dispels wind, lubricates the throat, helps improve vision, and clears congestion in the nose

Chinese Cabbage (Nappa) : *Sweet, neutral and slightly cold*

Nutritional Elements :

Calcium, potassium, phosphorus, folate, and vitamins A, C, B-6, and C

Therapeutic Actions :

Stomach and liver tonic, promotes digestion and urination, nourishes the kidneys and brain, cleans the stomach and intestines, relieves restlessness, and treats ulcers

Corn : *sweet, neutral*

Nutritional Elements :

Potassium, phosphorus, magnesium, folate, glutamic acid, aspartic acid, and vitamins A, B-6, and E

Therapeutic Actions:

Improves urination, nourishes the spleen, arrests bleeding, lowers blood pressure, reduces cholesterol, treats cardiovascular diseases

Chinese Prickly Ash : *pungent, warm*

Nutritional Elements :

Volatile oil, unsaturated organic acid

Therapeutic Actions :

Reinvigorates the stomach, removes worms, reduces inflammation, aids in tissue repair, and warms the body internally

Chives : *sweet, warm*

Nutritional Elements :

Calcium, potassium, manganese, volatile oil, sulfonium compound, protein, and vitamins A, B-6, E, and C

Therapeutic Actions :

Reinvigorates the stomach and kidneys, resolves extravagated blood that has leaked into tissues, improves digestion, detoxifies the body, treats impotence, relieves premature ejaculation, reduces inflammation of the intestines, and combats dysentery

Cucumber : *sweet, cold*

Nutritional Elements :

Niacin, protein, sugar, potassium and vitamins A, C, and E

Therapeutic Actions :

Clears away heat, quenches thirst, improves urination, removes swelling, lowers cholesterol, and reduces blood pressure

Eggplant : *sweet, cold*

Nutritional Elements :

Potassium, niacin, carotene, protein, and vitamins A, C, B-6, and E

Therapeutic Actions :

Resolves extravagated blood that has leaked into tissues, fights pain, removes swelling, protects capillaries, cleans intestines, treats cardiovascular diseases

Green Bean Sprouts : *sweet, cool*

Nutritional Elements :

Protein, potassium, folate, and vitamins C, A, and B-6

Therapeutic Actions :

Clears interior heat, stimulates the immune system, and relieves menstrual cramps

Hot Peppers (red and green) : *pungent, hot*

Nutritional Elements :

Capsaicin, capsicidin, potassium, manganese, protein, carotene, volatile oil, and vitamins A, C, B-6, and E

Therapeutic Actions :

Stimulates the production of saliva and stomach acid, combats a cold stomach, and treats rheumatic diseases

Note : *Hot peppers are counterproductive for chronic stomach diseases, tuberculosis, hypertension, toothaches, hemorrhoids, and swelling.*

Kelp : *salty, cold*

Nutritional Elements :

Iodine, calcium, magnesium, sodium, phosphorus, folate, carotene, protein, chlorophyll, iron, cobalt, and vitamins A, C, and E

Therapeutic Actions :

Softens hardness in the body, induces urination, replenishes blood, lowers cholesterol, treats enlargements of the thyroid gland, reduces hypertension, and treats vascular sclerosis, promotes circulation of body fluid

Note : *Kelp is particularly useful for treating cardiovascular diseases and diabetes.*

Leek : *pungent, warm*

Nutritional Elements :

Calcium, potassium, phosphorus, and vitamins C, B-6, A, and E

Therapeutic Actions :

Serves as a liver and lung tonic, removes blood stagnation, expels coldness, sedates yin, and clears interior heat

Note : *Leek can be irritating to some individuals and it is counter productive to eat leek if you suffer from stomach ailments, intestinal diseases, or cancer.*

Lotus Root : *sweet, cold when uncooked and warm when cooked*

Nutritional Elements :

Potassium, phosphorus, fiber, and vitamins C and B-6

Therapeutic Actions :

Uncooked (or rare) lotus root removes stasis, cools the blood, clears away heat, improves the appetite, and eliminates restlessness. Cooked lotus root nourishes the spleen and stomach

Mushroom : *sweet, cool*

Nutritional Elements :

Protein, potassium, phosphorus, amino acids, and vitamins D, B-6, E and C

Therapeutic Actions :

Nourishes the lungs, liver, stomach, spleen, and blood, clears heat, calms nerves, stimulates the appetite, resolves phlegm, lowers blood sugar, inhibits bacteria growth, treats decreased blood counts, combats cancer, and relieves chronic hepatitis

Potato : *sweet, neutral*

Nutritional Elements :

Starch, protein, potassium, lactic acid, citraconic acid, and vitamins B-6 and C

Therapeutic Actions :

Harmonizes the stomach, adjusts vital energy, reinvigorates the spleen, nourishes qi, reduces inflammation, fights stomach weakness, combats general fatigue, and relieves constipation

Pumpkin : *sweet, cold*

Nutritional Elements :

Potassium, folate, calcium, adenine, carotene, saccharose, and vitamins A, C and E

Therapeutic Actions :

Lubricates the lungs, replenishes vital energy, and restores qi

Radish : *pungent and sweet, slightly cold*

Nutritional Elements :

Calcium, phosphorus, folate, amylaceum, and vitamins B-6 and C

Therapeutic Actions :

Reinvigorates the stomach, improves digestion, relieves cough, resolves phlegm, soothes qi, improves urination, clears away internal heat, and detoxifies the body

Snow Peas : *sweet, neutral*

Nutritional Elements :

Potassium, magnesium, protein, fat, sugar, calcium, iron, folate, phosphorus, and vitamins C and A

Therapeutic Actions :

Improves urination, stops diarrhea, adjusts vital energy, reduces swelling, relieves hypertension, and treats other heart related diseases

Scallions : *pungent, warm*

Nutritional Elements :

Potassium, protein, carotene, calcium, iron, and vitamins A, C, B-6, and E

Therapeutic Actions :

Induces perspiration, relieves coldness, resolves phlegm, induces urination, improves digestion, improves appetite, and promotes blood circulation

Spinach : *sweet, cold*

Nutritional Elements :

Chlorophyll, magnesium, potassium, phosphorus, iron, oxalic acid, and vitamins A, B-6, E, and C

Therapeutic Actions :

Cleans intestines, replenishes and activates blood, quenches thirst, lubricates lungs, adjusts vital energy, improves digestion, reduces hypertension, treats constipation, and relieves hemorrhoids

Note : *Spinach should not be eaten if you suffer from stomach problems related to a cold stomach and/or you have loose bowels. Also, it is important to note that the oxalic acid in spinach reacts chemically with calcium, hampering the body's ability to absorb calcium. I suggest that you do not cook spinach with calcium-heavy food like beans, crab, or shrimp. If you do want to combine these ingredients be sure to boil the spinach for two minutes prior to combining them to remove the oxalic acid.*

Squash : *sweet, warm*

Nutritional Elements :

Calcium, magnesium, potassium, folate, betacarotene, and vitamins C and A

Therapeutic Actions :

Nourishes the spleen and stomach, replenishes yang, promotes blood circulation, resolves inflammation, and relieves pain

Chinese Yam : *sweet, neutral*

Nutritional Elements :

Amylase, potassium, phosphorus, folate, amino acids, and vitamins C, B-6, and E

Therapeutic Actions :

Nourishes the spleen and lungs, relieves cough, treats asthma, treats involuntary and frequent sperm emission, combats night sweats, relieves diarrhea, reduces involuntary discharge of urine and frequent urination, and eliminates abnormal female genital discharge

Taro : *sweet, neutral*

Nutritional Elements :

Calcium, magnesium, potassium, phosphorus, folate, and vitamins B-6, C, and E

Therapeutic Actions :

Nourishes the stomach and spleen, treats stomach disorders like ulcers and long-term constipation

Tomato : *sour and slightly sweet, neutral*

Nutritional Elements :

Protein, fat, sugar, calcium, potassium, phosphorus, magnesium,, iron, carotene, and vitamins A, E, and C

Therapeutic Actions :

Clears away internal heat, detoxifies the body, cools blood, and calms the liver

Towel Gourd : *sweet, neutral*

Nutritional Elements :

Calcium, magnesium, potassium, amino acids, sugar, fat, protein, and vitamins A, B-6, and C

Therapeutic Actions :

Clears heat from blood, detoxifies the body, relaxes the muscles, stimulates blood circulation, promotes the circulation of body fluid to remove swelling, induces a productive cough, reduces swelling, treats cardiovascular diseases, fights chronic respiratory system diseases, and relieves milk deficiency in new mothers

Turnip : *sweet, pungent, and bitter, neutral*

Nutritional Elements :

Calcium, phosphorus, potassium, sodium, folate, amylase, and vitamin C

Therapeutic Actions :

Invigorates yang, aids in blood circulation, clears interior heat, dries dampness, relieves water retention

Water Chestnut : *sweet, slightly cold*

Nutritional Elements :

Calcium, phosphorus, potassium, and vitamins C, E, and B-6

Therapeutic Actions :

Clears away internal heat, resolves phlegm, lowers blood pressure, treats chronic cough

White gourd : *sweet, slightly cold*

Nutritional Elements :

Calcium, potassium, oil, sugar, protein, niacin, and vitamins A and C

Therapeutic Actions :

Dispels dampness, clears heat, quenches thirst, improves urination, reduces swelling, relieves chest suppression, and treats kidney disease

Yellow Bean Sprouts : *sweet, cool*

Nutritional Elements :

Protein, phosphorus, calcium, magnesium, potassium, selenium, folate, and vitamins A and B-6

Therapeutic Actions :

Nourishes the spleen and stomach, clears blood vessels, removes swelling, reinvigorates the large intestine, reduces cholesterol, treats diabetes, and fights obesity

GRAINS

Barley : *salty, warm and slightly cold*

Nutritional Elements :

Malt sugar, amylaceum, calcium, magnesium, phosphorus, potassium, selenium, amylase, lecithinum, dextrin, and vitamins B-6 and A

Therapeutic Actions :

Nourishes qi, adjusts vital energy, improves digestion, treats severe indigestion and abdominal distension, and promotes urination

Millet : *sweet, slightly cold*

Nutritional Elements :

Calcium, magnesium, phosphorus, potassium, niacin, protein, fatty acids, sugar, and vitamins B-6 and E

Therapeutic Actions :

Harmonizes the stomach, calms restlessness, alleviates sleeplessness, and improves weak digestion

Wheat bran : *sweet, slightly cold*

Nutritional Elements :

Fiber, protein, fatty acids, calcium, magnesium, phosphorus, potassium, selenium, niacin, folate, and vitamins B-6 and E

Therapeutic Actions :

Calms restlessness, alleviates sweating and night sweats due to body deficiencies, and relieves extreme thirst

White rice : *sweet, neutral*

Nutritional Elements :

Starch, protein, phosphorus, potassium, selenium, folate, and vitamin B-6

Therapeutic Actions :

Nourishes the spleen and stomach

LEGUMES

Black Soybean : *sweet, neutral*

Nutritional Elements :

Fat, protein, calcium, phosphorus, potassium, selenium, folate, niacin, and vitamins A, E, B-6, and C

Therapeutic Actions :

Adjusts vital energy, replenishes qi, promotes circulation of body fluid, reduces swelling, eliminates toxins, treats fever, and alleviates night sweats that are caused by fatigue

Note : *Black soybeans are high in protein and should not be eaten if you suffer from gout.*

Mung Beans : *sweet, cold*

Nutritional Elements :

Calcium, phosphorus, potassium, folate, and vitamins A, C, and B-6

Therapeutic Actions :

Promotes the circulation of body fluids, reduces swelling, clears away excessive body heat, detoxifies the body, treats throat pain, relieves constipation

Red Beans : *sweet and sour, neutral*

Nutritional Elements :

Starch, protein, sugar, calcium, magnesium, potassium, phosphorus, folate and vitamins A, B-6, and C

Therapeutic Actions :

Clears away excessive body heat, improves urination, removes swelling, and resolves extravagated or pooled blood

Soybeans : *salty, cold*

Nutritional Elements :

Protein, fat, calcium, potassium, folate, iron, and vitamins C and A

Therapeutic Actions :

Nourishes large intestines, removes swelling, detoxifies the body, and lowers cholesterol

Soy Sauce : *salty, cold*

Nutritional Elements :

Protein, calcium, potassium, sodium, phosphorus, amino acids, niacin, and vitamin B-6

Therapeutic Actions :

Clears excessive body heat and calms restlessness

String Beans : *sweet, slightly warm*

Nutritional Elements :

Calcium, potassium, phosphorus, amino acids, and vitamins A, B-6, and C

Therapeutic Actions :

Harmonizes vital energy, reinvigorates the stomach, clears away heat, treats stomach and spleen deficiencies, relieves diarrhea and vomiting caused by a vital energy disorder such as an acute inflammation of the intestines

Sword Beans : *sweet, neutral*

Nutrition Elements :

Protein, fat, lecithinum

Therapeutic Actions :

Adjusts vital energy, nourishes the kidneys and the stomach, and alleviates vomiting

Note : *Sword beans are high in protein and should be avoided if you suffer from gout.*

Tofu : *sweet and salty, cold and neutral*

Nutritional Elements :

Protein, fat, calcium, potassium, niacin, amino acids, and vitamins A and B-6

Therapeutic Actions :

Nourishes yin, relieves dryness, harmonizes the stomach and qi, clears away heat, replenishes blood, removes blood stasis, promotes the production of milk, improves the circulation of body fluids, reduces swelling, treats cardiovascular diseases, combats diabetes, and fights obesity

NUTS

Lotus Seed : *sweet, neutral*

Nutritional Elements :

Calcium, phosphorus, potassium, folate, and vitamin A

Therapeutic Actions :

Restores vital energy, strengthens the spleen, arrests dysentery, restricts excessive or involuntary seminal emission, treats heart palpitations, relieves insomnia, reduces fatigue, combats chronic dysentery, and eliminates abnormal female genital discharge

Sesame Seeds : *sweet, neutral*

Nutritional Elements :

Calcium, magnesium, phosphorus, sodium, oleic acid, protein, and vitamins A and E

Therapeutic Actions :

Lubricates the intestines, harmonizes blood, nourishes the liver and kidney, darkens hair, alleviates fatigue due to kidney deficiency, treats anemia, combats constipation, relieves dizziness, and fights tinnitus

HERBS

Coriander : *pungent, warm*

Nutritional Elements :

Fat, fiber, calcium, iron, magnesium, phosphorus, selenium, potassium, and vitamin C

Therapeutic Actions :

Relieves rashes, promotes blood circulation, dispels coldness and wind, removes odor, acts as a lung and stomach tonic, alleviates the symptoms of measles, detoxifies the body, and fights the growth of bacteria and fungus

Dried Ginger : *pungent, hot*

Nutritional Elements :

Starch, ginserols, calcium, magnesium, potassium, selenium, and vitamin A

Therapeutic Actions :

Works as a lung, stomach and spleen tonic, helps blood circulation, warms the interior, lubricates the lungs, resolves phlegm, alleviates a cough, removes toxins from the body, improves digestion, and reduces vomiting

Ginger : *pungent, slightly warm*

Nutritional Elements :

Phytosterols, calcium, potassium, and volatile oil

Therapeutic Actions :

Induces sweat, warms the interior, eliminates vomiting, detoxifies the body, treats flu symptoms, alleviates a cold spleen and stomach caused by deficiencies, relieves water retention, and promotes blood circulation

Garlic : *pungent, warm*

Nutritional Elements :

Protein, calcium, potassium, and vitamins B-6 and C

Therapeutic Actions :

Soothes qi, expels wind and coldness, detoxifies the body, dispels worms, arrests loose bowels, improves urination, lowers blood pressure, arrests bleeding, removes phlegm, diminishes inflammation, reinvigorates the stomach, induces the production of stomach acid, lowers blood pressure and cholesterol, and resolves extravagated blood

Note : *Those who have any kind of a stomach disease should avoid garlic.*

Ginseng : *Sweet and slightly bitter, slightly warm*

Nutritional Elements :

Polysaccharides, ginsenosides

Therapeutic Actions :

Invigorates qi, nourishes the spleen and lungs, promotes the production of body fluid, quenches thirst, calms the mind, reduces shortness of breath, relieves mental fatigue, combats fainting, reduces excessive bleeding, alleviates vomiting and diarrhea, stimulates a poor appetite, reduces fatigue, reduces perspiration, and strengthens a weak pulse resulting from severe or chronic illnesses

FRUIT

Apple : *sour, neutral*

Nutritional Elements :

Potassium, apple acid, tannin, sugar, fiber, and vitamins A and C

Therapeutic Actions :

Nourishes the heart, replenishes qi, quenches thirst by promoting salivation, reinvigorates the stomach, harmonizes the spleen, stops diarrhea, treats indigestion, and relieves constipation

Apricot : *sweet and sour, warm*

Nutritional Elements :

Sugar, calcium, potassium, iron, vitamins A, B-6, E, and C

Therapeutic Actions :

Lubricates the intestines and improves digestion

Note : *Apricots should be eaten in moderation because in certain people they can irritate the teeth, stomach, and intestines.*

Chinese Red Date : *sweet, neutral*

Nutritional Elements :

Protein, sugar, potassium, calcium, and vitamins B-6 and E

Therapeutic Actions :

Nourishes the spleen and stomach, relieves restlessness, and treats anemia and hepatitis

Note : *Chinese Red Date is a particularly useful food during the menstrual cycle and after giving birth.*

Pomegranate (Granada) : *sweet, warm*

Nutritional Elements :

Sugar, tannin, potassium, and vitamin C

Therapeutic Actions :

Acts as an antibiotic, treats dysentery, relieves inflammation of the intestines, fights gallbladder disease, combats lung infections, and eliminates boils

Grapes (red and green) : *sweet, neutral*

Nutritional Elements :

Sugar, potassium, niacin, and vitamins B-6, A, E and C

Therapeutic Actions :

Replenishes vital energy, dispels wind and coldness, improves urination, stimulates a poor appetite caused by fatigue or deficiencies

Hawthorn Fruit : *sweet and sour, slightly warm*

Nutrition Elements :

Crataegin, tannin, fruit sugar, fruit acid, pectin, and vitamin C

Therapeutic Actions :

Improves digestion (particularly of meat), fights dysentery, reduces blood pressure, dilates blood vessels, reduces cholesterol, alleviates abdominal pain after giving birth

Peach : *sweet and sour, cool*

Nutritional Elements :

Volatile oil, potassium, and vitamins C and A

Therapeutic Actions :

Resolves extravagated or pooled blood, lubricates intestines, calms coughs, alleviates painful menstruation, reduces hypertension, combats lung diseases, and treats traumatic injuries

Pear : *sweet and slightly sour, cold*

Nutritional Elements :

Fructopyranose, amylaceum, organic acid, potassium carotene, and vitamins B-6 and C

Therapeutic Actions :

Lubricates lungs, stops cough, resolves phlegm, clears interior heat, and lowers blood pressure

Note : *Eat pears in moderation because too much pear can induce dampness in the body, which can harm the spleen and stomach.*

Persimmon : *sweet, cold*

Nutritional Elements :

Potassium, calcium, tannic acid, and vitamin A

Therapeutic Actions :

Promotes the production of body fluids, lubricates the lungs, astringes the intestines, and lowers blood pressure

Note : *Avoid eating persimmons on an empty stomach and do not eat them during recuperation after illness, after giving birth, or if you are anemic.*

Tangerine : *sweet and sour, warm*

Nutritional Elements :

Amylaceum, potassium, and vitamins C and A

Therapeutic Actions :

Reinvigorates the stomach, soothes qi, relieves cough, resolves phlegm, treats gas stagnation in the stomach and spleen, reduces fever, alleviates indigestion, treats chronic cardiovascular diseases like hypertension and coronary disease

Watermelon : *sweet, cold*

Nutritional Elements :

Orthophosphoric acid, apple acid, fructopyranose, amylaceum, amino acids, carotene, potassium, and vitamins C and A

Therapeutic Actions :

Relieves chest congestion, alleviates thirst, eliminates throat aches, combats brown urine, alleviates canker sores, and combats the coughing up of blood due to interior heat.

Note : *Eating too much watermelon can result in interior dampness and cold.*

MISCELLANEOUS FOODS

Brown sugar : *sweet, warm*

Nutritional Elements :

Potassium, calcium, and iron

Therapeutic Actions :

Warms the interior, promotes the circulation of blood to remove stasis, treats stomach problems, useful during the menstrual cycle and after giving birth

Honey : *sweet, neutral*

Nutritional Elements :

Amylaceum, saccharose, dextrin, organic acid, niacin, potassium, and vitamins B-6 and C

Therapeutic Actions :

Restores deficiencies, moistens lungs, strengthens the stomach and spleen, stops pain and detoxifies body, treats abdominal pain due to spleen and stomach deficiencies, relieves the symptoms of asthma, eliminates an unproductive cough, combats constipation, treats cardiovascular disease, fights anemia, treats ulcers, fights eye diseases and liver diseases, relieves the symptoms of arthritis, nourishes the heart muscles, protects the liver, and lowers blood pressure

Tea : *sweet and bitter, slight cold*

Nutritional Elements :

Potassium, manganese, theanine, and volatile oil

Therapeutic Actions :

Clears interior heat, calms the mind, improves digestion, awakens nerves, improves urination, detoxifies the body, lowers cholesterol, reduces inflammation of the intestines, fights arteriosclerosis and reduces hypertension

Note : *Tea should be avoided if you are constipated and by women who are lactating as it may restrict milk production.*

Vinegar : *Sour and bitter, warm*

Nutritional Elements :

Potassium, magnesium, sthylic acid, sugar, aldehyde, and sodium

Therapeutic Actions :

Strengthens the stomach, improves digestion, kills or restrains bacteria, treats intestinal worms, prevents vitamin C loss, aids in the absorption of calcium, treats ringworm, and fights diseases of the respiratory system, hypertension, and arteriosclerosis

White sugar (granulated) : *Sweet, cool*

Nutritional Elements :

Calcium, zinc, copper, phosphorous, potassium, iron, manganese, selenium, riboflavin

Therapeutic Actions :

Lubricates the lungs and clears away internal body heat

Note : *Sugar can cause a number of diseases to progress and should always be used in moderation.*

Wine : *Sweet and pungent, warm-hot*

Nutritional Elements :

Calcium, iron, magnesium, phosphorus, potassium, folate, vitamin B-6 and niacin

Therapeutic Actions :

Promotes blood circulation, expels coldness from the body, fights heart disease, and accelerates the healing properties in herbs

Note : *Drinking too much alcohol can severely harm your health. As always, moderation is the key.*

APPENDIX II

Healing From the Inside Out: Foods to Eat and Avoid

Use this helpful quick chart to identify which foods to eat and which foods to avoid (when applicable)for fifteen of the most common complaints and illnesses that I address in my healing practice every day.

Food and Common Illnesses

Fever

Foods to Eat

Plain foods. Noodles, rice, fresh vegetables, sugar cane, oranges, and other fresh fruits.

Foods to Avoid

Oily, deep-fried, and pungent foods.

Senior chronic bronchitis

Foods to Eat

Plain and easily digested, high-calorie and high-vitamin foods. Eel, soft-shelled turtle, kelp, radishes, water chestnuts, and fresh greens.

Foods to Avoid

Alcohol, smoked, oily and pungent foods.

High cholesterol, hypertension, and coronary diseases

Foods to Eat

Plain foods. Rice, wheat flour, corn. Fresh greens, beans, melons, kelp. Vegetable oil. Water chestnuts, hawthorn fruit, persimmon, and bee honey.

Foods to Avoid

High-fat, high-cholesterol and pungent foods. Fatty meats, organ meats, egg yolk, roe, alcohol, strong tea, and coffee.

Liver diseases : Acute hepatitis

Foods to Eat

Plain foods. Moderate amounts of milk, eggs, fish, beans and bean products like tofu and soy-milk. Sugar, jam, honey, and other high calorie foods. Vegetables with strong vitamin content such as greens, bean sprouts, tomatoes, and various melons.

Foods to Avoid

Pungent foods. Alcohol. Minimize salt intake. Beans, potatoes, and sweet potatoes.

Liver diseases : Chronic hepatitis

Foods to Eat

Fresh vegetables, tofu, jam, fish and sweet congees (rice porridges).

Foods to Avoid

Pungent foods. Alcohol. Minimize salt intake. Beans, potatoes, and sweet potatoes

Cholecystitis (chronic inflammation of the bladder)

Foods to Eat

Fresh vegetables like greens, radishes and turnips. Edible wild herbs, tomatoes, and melons. Fresh fruits.

Foods to Avoid

High-cholesterol, fatty, deep-fried, and pungent foods.

Stomach diseases : Acute gastritis

Foods to Eat

In the beginning limit yourself to only liquid or half-liquid foods like vegetable and fruit juices. Easily-digested foods can then be added back into the diet.

Foods to Avoid

Alcohol, strong tea or coffee, pungent foods, deep-fried foods, cold, and hard foods.

Stomach diseases : Chronic gastritis

Foods to Eat

Easily digested foods with high vitamin B, protein, and iron content.

Foods to Avoid

Alcohol, strong tea or coffee, pungent foods, deep-fried foods, cold, and hard foods.

Stomach diseases : Gastroduodenal ulcer

Foods to Eat

Easily digested food such as congees, bean products, and greens.

Foods to Avoid

Alcohol, strong tea or coffee, pungent foods, deep-fried foods, cold, and hard foods.

Stomach diseases : Ptosis of the stomach

Foods to Eat

Nutritious but easily digested foods such as sticky-rice, congee, eggs, milk, lean meat, fish, chicken, pork liver, and greens.

Foods to Avoid

Alcohol, strong tea or coffee, pungent foods, deep-fried foods, cold, and hard foods.

Diabetes

Foods to Eat

Low sugar fruits like kiwi and bananas. Low-starch foods. Fresh vegetables like cabbage, chives, radishes, tomatoes, and carrots.

Foods to Avoid

Sugar, jam, and honey. Large amounts of wheat flour, potatoes, and lotus roots.

Tuberculosis

Foods to Eat

High calorie foods rich in proteins, calcium, and vitamins such as meats, milk, eggs, fish, fresh vegetables and fruits. Goat milk.

Foods to Avoid

Alcohol. Smoked, oily, and pungent foods.

Anemia

Foods to Eat

Foods with high iron content. Some animal organs like liver. Lean meats, eggs, milk, soybeans. Vegetables especially spinach and tomatoes. Fruits like pineapples, dates, apricots, peaches, oranges, and tangerines.

Foods to Avoid

None.

Chronic constipation

Foods to Eat

Fresh fruits like pears and apples. Fresh vegetables like celery. Foods that can create gas such as onions, soybeans, and radishes. Plenty of water.

Foods to Avoid

Pungent and hot foods.

Kidney diseases : Acute kidney disorders

Foods to Eat

Sugar congees, vegetables, fruits, jams, and honey. Low salt foods and high protein foods.

Foods to Avoid

Greasy foods, deep-fried and cold foods. Garlic, scallions, chives and hot peppers. Alcohol.

Kidney diseases : Chronic kidney disorders

Foods to Eat

Low salt foods, easily digested foods. Fruits. Vegetables like white gourd, squash, bamboo shoots, greens, and radishes.

Foods to Avoid

Greasy foods, deep-fried and cold foods. Garlic, scallions, chives and hot peppers. Alcohol.

Skin diseases

Foods to Eat

Towel gourd. Plain foods.

Foods to Avoid

Yellow fish, crab, shrimp, mushrooms, bamboo shoots, and chives.

Cancer : Skin cancer, matrix cancer, prostate cancer, breast cancer

Foods to Eat

Plain foods. Vegetables, fruits, nuts, and seeds.

Foods to Avoid

Seafood, mushrooms, bamboo shoots, and chives. All pungent foods.

Cancer : Liver cancer, lung cancer, stomach cancer

Foods to Eat

Vegetarian foods, organic foods, nuts, and seeds.

Foods to Avoid

Seafood, mushrooms, bamboo shoots, and chives. All pungent foods.

Arthritis

Foods to Eat

Moderately pungent foods like ginger and hot pepper.

Foods to Avoid

Eggplant, tomato, and potatoes.

Alzheimer's

Foods to Eat

Eat less (smaller portions) to accelerate toxic discharge from the body.

Foods to Avoid

None.

APPENDIX III

Daily Diet Plans

Here a more in-depth look is given to some of the most common illnesses plaguing the Western world today. Specific advice is offered for each ailment, and each is accompanied by a disease-specific daily diet plan.

Please note that I have not included a daily diet plan for arthritis. A true arthritis diet plan that would cover all the different types of arthritis would be impossible to address in the space I have here. If you do suffer from arthritis or painful joints you will find a number of recipes throughout the book that may help to relieve your symptoms. Experiment to find out which ones work the best for you.

"High blood pressure can develop over many years with no noticeable symptoms. Warning signs can include nosebleeds, a racing or an irregular heartbeat, headaches, and dizziness."

Hypertension

Keeping your blood pressure under control is tremendously important to your overall health. High blood pressure is one of several factors associated with cardiovascular disease, which is the number 1 killer of United States citizens—both men and women. Cardiovascular disease claims more lives annually than all cancers combined, killing approximately 1 million people in the United States each year. It disables countless others.

The cause of high blood pressure is unknown in 90 percent of all cases. This is called "essential hypertension." In secondary hypertension, a disease or other physical problem is behind the diagnosis. Common causes are kidney disease and thyroid disease. Many factors are associated with high blood pressure, including genetics, age, race, stress, obesity, smoking, a high-salt diet, excessive consumption of alcohol, and a sedentary lifestyle.

High blood pressure can develop over many years with no noticeable symptoms. Warning signs can include nosebleeds, a racing or an irregular heartbeat, headaches, and dizziness.

To control blood pressure, you should do the following:

» Have your blood pressure checked regularly. Your primary care physician can tell you how often.

» Stop smoking.

» Avoid excessive salt intake. If you are sensitive to sodium excessive salt can make high blood pressure worse. Salt can cause water retention, which makes your heart work harder than it has to. The National High Blood Pressure Education Program recommends no more than 2,400 milligrams per day (the amount in about 1 teaspoon of table salt).

» Eat more fresh fruits, vegetables, and foods high in fiber and low in fat. High-fiber foods include tofu and other bean products. Seafood (except some with high cholesterol, such as shrimp and crab), chicken, and duck are also acceptable.

» Reduce stress on and off the job; master relaxation techniques.

» Practice moderation when drinking alcohol.

» Exercise regularly and keep your weight within normal limits.

Suggested foods for hypertension:

Breakfast :
Oatmeal or grits, soymilk, yogurt, tea, low-fat or fat-free milk, fruit

Lunch :
Vegetable or fruit salad, nuts, rice, vegetables, noodles, bean products, fish, chicken

Dinner :
Bean products, vegetables, soups, chicken, fish, beef, lamb, and pork

"Cardiovascular disease claims more lives annually than all cancers combined, killing approximately 1 million people in the United States each year. It disables countless others."

» If your doctor prescribes medication to lower your blood pressure, be sure to follow his or her directions exactly.

Master Hou's Advice:

» Eat meat no more than three times a week.

» Eat more than 1.5 pounds of vegetables and more than 1 pound of fruit each day.

» Eat plant proteins when possible (such as mushrooms, wheat flour, and soybean products).

» Drink more tea especially herbal varieties.

» Drink at least 6 glasses of carrot juice each week.

» Try to eat only well done meats (avoid rare meats).

» Fish should not be eaten more than 3 times a week.

Diet Plan for a Week

Follow this plan for two months. Please note that dishes and beverages can be varied based on the general principles above. This plan is provided as a guideline. Corresponding page numbers are provided for the specific recipes mentioned in the book.

MONDAY

Breakfast

Oatmeal or grits, 1 bowl

Sweet and Sour Cucumbers (page 165), 1 dish

Chrysanthemum Tea (page 33) or green tea, 1 cup

Wheat bread, 1 slice

Lunch

Vegetable salad (may include chicken and nuts), 1 dish

Vegetable Rice Casserole (page 223) or wheat bread, 1 dish or 1 slice

Chrysanthemum Tea (page 33) or green tea, 1 cup

Dinner

Gingered Carp (page 139), 1 dish

Chinese Cabbage With Mushrooms (page 150), 1 dish

Pork Spareribs With Kelp Soup (page 54), 1 bowl

Fruit (apple, orange, or banana), 1 piece

TUESDAY

Breakfast

Golden Fried Wheat Flour Tea (page 38), 1 dish

Orange juice or green tea, 1 glass or 1 cup

Fruit (apple or banana), 1 piece

Lunch

Steamed Spinach Noodles (page 228), 1 plate

Vegetable salad, 1 dish

Dinner

Tofu with Minced Pork (page 94), 1 dish

Mushrooms With Garlic (page 154), 1 dish

Fruit (orange, apple, banana, or kiwi), 1 piece

WEDNESDAY

Breakfast

Oatmeal or grits, 1 bowl

Bitter Melon With Soybeans (page 162), 1 dish

Fresh carrot juice, 1 glass

Lunch

Spicy Gingered Chicken (page 106), 1 dish

Sandwich (chicken or tuna), 1 piece

Tea (lemon tea), 1 cup

Dinner

Spinach and Pork Soup (page 67), 1 bowl

Tofu With Green Onion (page 171), 1 dish

String Beans in Ginger Dressing (page 176), 1 dish

Fruit (orange, apple, banana, or kiwi.), 1 piece

THURSDAY

Breakfast

Soy milk plus an egg white, 1 glass

Cucumber With Coriander and Hot Green Pepper (page 167), 1 dish

Bread, 1 small slice

Tea or black coffee, 1 cup

Lunch

White Rice Congee (page 220), 1 bowl

Scallop Fried Rice (page 222), 1 dish

Fruit (orange, apple, banana, or kiwi), 1 piece

Dinner

Hot Green Pepper With Potato Strips (page 191), 1 dish

Spicy Gingered Chicken (page 106), 1 dish

Chinese Cabbage and Tofu Soup (page 73), 1 bowl

Chrysanthemum Tea (page 33) or green tea, 1 cup

FRIDAY

Breakfast

Soy-milk or White Rice Congee (page 220), 1 glass or 1 bowl

Sesame Spinach and Celery (page 173), 1 dish

Wheat bread, 1 slice

Chrysanthemum Tea (page 33) or green tea, 1 cup

Lunch

Sandwich (chicken or tuna), 1 piece

Vegetable salad, 1 dish

Fresh carrot juice, 1 glass

Dinner

Savory Lamb With Sweet and Tangy Carrots (page 84), 1 dish

Peanuts and Celery (page 187), 1 dish

Rice or wheat bread, optional

Carrot juice, 1 glass

Bamboo Shoots and Tofu Soup (page 48), 1 bowl

SATURDAY

Breakfast

Oatmeal or grits, 1 bowl

Simple Spiced-up Celery (page 172), 1 dish

Lunch

Pork Chow Mein (page 226), 1 dish

Fruit (orange, apple, banana, or kiwi), 1 piece

Chrysanthemum Tea (page 33) or green tea, 1 cup

Dinner

Jellyfish and Turnip (page 140), 1 dish

Green Bell Pepper With Green Bean Sprouts (179), 1 dish

Soybean and Pork Spareribs Soup (page 66), 1 bowl

Chrysanthemum Tea (page 33) or green tea, 1 cup

SUNDAY

Breakfast & lunch

Golden Fried Wheat Flour Tea (page 38), 1 glass

Fruit juice, 1 glass

Stewed Lamb Rice (page 224), 1 dish

Dinner

Tomato and Pork Soup (page 69), 1 bowl

Vegetable salad, 1 dish

Fish Fillet With Garlic and Ginger Cucumbers (page 136), 1 dish

Wheat bread, 2 slices

Diabetes

According to the National Institute of Health 15.7 million Americans, almost 6 percent of the U.S. population, have diabetes. There are approximately 798,000 new cases diagnosed a year—and hundreds of thousands that go tragically undiagnosed.

Diabetes is a quiet killer that can cause serious health problems. It is the leading cause of adult blindness, kidney failure, and non-traumatic amputations. Those suffering from diabetes have a 2 to 4 times higher risk of having a stroke or dieing from heart disease. And if you're a diabetic you have a 60 percent to 65 percent chance of having high blood pressure. So far there is no cure. Diabetes can be controlled, however, through diet, exercise, and medication.

"Diabetes is a quiet killer that can cause serious health problems. It is the leading cause of adult blindness, kidney failure, and non-traumatic amputations."

When people eat, food is normally digested and much of it is converted to glucose—a simple sugar that the body uses for energy. The blood carries the glucose to cells, where it is absorbed with the help of the hormone insulin. For those with diabetes, however, the body does not make enough or cannot properly use the insulin it does make. Without insulin, glucose accumulates in the blood

Suggested foods for diabetes:

Breakfast:
Oatmeal or grits, soy-milk, low-fat or fat-free milk, fruit

Lunch:
Vegetables, fruit that is low in sugar, salad, nuts, rice, bean products, fish, chicken

Dinner:
Bean products, fish, vegetables, soups, chicken, beef, lamb, and pork

instead of moving into the cells resulting in high blood-sugar levels.

There are two major types of diabetes: Type I, sometimes called juvenile onset or insulin-dependent diabetes, and Type II, often referred to as adult-onset or non-insulin-dependent diabetes.

Those with Type I diabetes must take insulin to utilize glucose and avoid ketoacidosis, a life-threatening condition that occurs when the body burns fat for energy instead of glucose. Type I diabetes is more common in whites than in other ethnic groups.

Type II diabetes is the more common form of diabetes in the United States, accounting for more than 90 percent of all cases. The risk factors of Type II include obesity, unfavorable body-fat distribution, and inactivity. People with Type II control their condition by limiting the type and amount of food they eat and by exercising. It is more common among Hispanics, Native-Americans, African-Americans, Alaskan natives, Pacific Islanders, and those of Asian ancestry than among Caucasians.

Master Hou's advice:

» Eat foods that are low in sugar.

» Eat less wheat flour, as it contains a lot of starch that can be converted into sugar. Eat no more than three wheat-flour dishes per week and be sure each dish contains no more than 7 ounces of wheat flour.

» Rice, oatmeal, and grits are acceptable foods.

» Meat and seafood in moderation are acceptable.

» Eat at least 2 pounds of vegetables a day. Vegetables like cauliflower, cabbage, and green pepper are ideal foods for diabetics.

» Eat lower sugar fruits, such as bananas and kiwis.

» Diabetics may feel hungry more often than other people. When hunger strikes try eating more vegetables.

"Diabetes can be controlled, however, through diet, exercise, and medication."

Diet plan for a week

Follow this plan for two months. Please note that dishes and beverages can be varied based on the general principles above. This plan is provided as a guideline. Corresponding page numbers are provided for the specific recipes mentioned in the book.

MONDAY

Breakfast

Soy milk or fat-free milk, 1 glass
Sesame Spinach (page 163), 1 dish
Chrysanthemum Tea (page 33) or green tea, 1 cup

Lunch

Sweet and Sour Crisp-skin Crucian Fish (page 138), 1 dish
Vegetable salad (may include chicken and nuts), 1 dish

Dinner

Pork Spareribs With Kelp Soup (page 54), 1 bowl
Stewed Lamb Rice (page 224), 1 dish
Cucumber With Garlic (page 166), 1 dish

TUESDAY

Breakfast

Soy milk or fat-free milk plus 1-2 egg whites, 1 glass
Vegetable salad, 1 dish
Chrysanthemum Tea (page 33) or green tea, 1 cup

Lunch

Pork With Asparagus Lettuce (page 96), 1 dish
Chinese Cabbage With Mushrooms (page 150), 1 dish
Brown or white rice, 1 bowl

Dinner

Tofu With Minced Pork (page 94), 1 dish
Mushrooms With Garlic (page 154), 1 dish
A low-sugar fruit (banana, kiwi, or avocado), 1 piece

WEDNESDAY

Breakfast

Oatmeal or grits, 1 bowl
Vegetable salad, 1 dish
Bread, 1 small slice

Lunch

Sandwich (chicken or tuna), 1 piece
Your choice of a vegetable, 1 dish

Dinner

Inkfish With Garlic and Chives (page 127), 1 dish
Stewed Lean Pork With Mushrooms (page 102), 1 dish
Hearty Pork, Tofu, and Towel Gourd Soup (page 70), 1 bowl

THURSDAY

Breakfast

Soy milk plus one egg white, 1 glass
Vegetable salad, 1 dish
Chrysanthemum Tea (page 33) or green tea, 1 cup

Lunch

Brown or white rice, 1 dish
Seared Beef With Turnip (page 100), 1 dish
Crisp and Hot Cucumber Strips (page 202), 1 dish

Dinner

Chinese Cabbage and Tofu Soup (page 73), 1 bowl
Shrimp With Steamed Egg and Garden Fresh Vegetables Soup (page 112), 1 dish
Hot Green Pepper With Bitter Melon (page 174), 1 dish
Chrysanthemum Tea (page 33) or green tea, 1 cup

FRIDAY

Breakfast

Soy milk plus one egg white, 1 glass
Vegetable salad, 1 dish
Chrysanthemum Tea (page 33), or green tea, or black coffee, 1 cup

Lunch

Fortune Fried Rice (page 221), 1 dish
Green Bell Pepper With Green Bean Sprouts (page 179), 1 dish

Dinner

Sautéed Lamb (page 100), 1 dish
Hot Green Pepper With Bitter Melon (page 174), 1 dish
Delicious Dynasty Soup (page 51), 1 bowl
A low-sugar fruit (banana, kiwi, or avocado), 1 piece

SATURDAY

Breakfast

Soy milk plus one egg white, 1 glass
Vegetable salad, 1 dish
A low-sugar fruit (banana, kiwi, or avocado), 1 piece
Chrysanthemum Tea (page 33), or green tea, or black coffee, 1 cup

Lunch

Sandwich (chicken or tuna), 1 sandwich
Bamboo Shoots With Green Onions (page 193), 1 dish
Spicy Gingered Chicken (page 106), 1 dish

Dinner

Savory Eggplant Strip Sauté (page 202), 1 dish
Butterfish With Garlic (page 122), 1 dish
Sesame Spinach (page 163), 1 dish

SUNDAY

Breakfast and lunch

Mushroom and Snow Peas Soup (page 61), 1 bowl

Fiery Pork Strips With Squash (page 92), 1 dish

Brown or white rice, 1 dish

Dinner

Fresh Corn With Hot Green Pepper (page 157), 1 dish

Simple Spiced-up Celery (page 172), 1 dish

Soybean and Pork Spareribs Soup (page 66), 1 bowl

Suggested foods for weight reduction:

Breakfast:

Soy-milk, low-fat or fat-free milk, and fruit

Lunch:

Vegetable or low-sugar fruit salad, nuts, rice, bean products, fish, chicken

Dinner:

bean products, vegetables, soups, chicken, fish

Weight loss/Obesity

Over one-half of all Americans (about 97 million) are overweight with nearly one quarter of U.S. adults being considered obese. If you are carrying this extra weight you are at risk for developing many diseases, including heart disease, stroke, diabetes, and cancer. Losing the extra weight helps to prevent and control those diseases. The following guidelines, when combined with regular exercise, can provide you with a new approach for safe and effective weight loss.

Master Hou's advice:

» Follow a low calorie diet for weight loss. Reducing fat is a practical way to reduce calories.

» Physical activity should be an integral part of weight loss therapy and weight maintenance.

» Daily vegetable consumption should not be less than 3 pounds. Eat only one meat dish a day.

» Eat high fiber foods, especially raw vegetables.

» Do not eat overeat at meals and avoid snacking between meals.

» Drink water instead of other drinks.

Diet plan for a week:

Follow this plan for two months. Please note that dishes and beverages can be varied based on the general principles above. This plan is provided as a guideline. Corresponding page numbers are provided for the specific recipes mentioned in the book.

MONDAY

Breakfast

Soy milk plus two egg whites, 1 glass
Vegetable salad, 1 dish
Green tea, 1 cup

Lunch

Sandwich (chicken or tuna), 1 sandwich
Simple Spiced-up Celery (page 172), 1 dish

Dinner

Green Bean Sprouts With Chives (page 180), 1 dish
Spicy Bite Radishes (page 195), 1 dish
Wheat bread, 1 slice

TUESDAY

Breakfast

Soy milk plus two egg whites, 1 glass
A low-sugar fruit (banana or kiwi), 1 piece

Lunch

Vegetable Rice Casserole (page 223), 1 dish
Vegetable salad, 1 dish

Dinner

Tofu in Tomato Sauce (page 170), 1 dish
Sweet and Sour Cucumbers (page 165), 1 dish
Wheat bread, 2 slices

WEDNESDAY

Breakfast

Fat-free milk, 1 glass

Vegetable salad, 1 dish

Lunch

Chinese Cabbage in Vinegar (page 147), 1 dish

Shrimp With Cauliflower (page 115), 1 dish

Brown or white rice, 1 dish

Dinner

Wok-fried Tomatoes (page 153), 1 dish

Salty Shrimp (page 117), 1 dish

Chinese Broccoli Sauté (page 196), 1 dish

THURSDAY

Breakfast

Soy milk plus one egg white, 1 glass

Vegetable salad, 1 dish

Chrysanthemum Tea (page 33) or green tea, 1 cup

Lunch

Brown or white rice, 1 dish

Pork Strips With Celery and Carrot (page 95), 1 dish

Cucumber with Garlic (page 166), 1 dish

Dinner

Turnips and Crushed Garlic (page 168), 1 dish

Sour Noodle Soup (page 65), 1 dish

Vegetable salad, 1 dish

Chrysanthemum Tea (page 33), 1 cup

FRIDAY

Breakfast

Soy milk plus one egg white, 1 glass
Avocado and Tofu With Tomato Salad (page 161), 1 dish
Wheat bread, 1 slice

Lunch

Fish Fillet With Garlic and Ginger Cucumbers (page 136), 1 dish
Simple Spiced-up Celery (page 172), 1 dish
A low-sugar fruit (banana or kiwi), 1 piece

Dinner

Tofu in Tomato Sauce (page 170), 1 dish
Pork Spareribs With Kelp Soup (page 54), 1 bowl
Bitter Melon in Red- pepper Oil (page 175), 1 dish

SATURDAY

Breakfast

Soy milk plus one egg white, 1 glass
Vegetable salad, 1 dish
A low-sugar fruit (banana or kiwi), 1 piece
Chrysanthemum Tea (page 33) or green tea, or black coffee, 1 cup

Lunch

Sandwich (chicken or tuna), 1 sandwich
Spicy Gingered Chicken (page 106), 1 dish
Sweet and Sour Cucumbers (page 165), 1 dish

Dinner

Spicy Sautéed Conch (page 137), 1 dish
Savory Spiced Turnip and Lamb Soup (page 71), 1 bowl
Sesame Spinach (page 163), 1 dish
Brown or white rice, 1 bowl

SUNDAY

Breakfast and lunch

White-gourd Sauté (page 215), 1 dish

Eggs with Cucumber (page 158), 1 dish

Wheat bread, 2 slices

Dinner

Savory Eggplant Strip Sauté (page 202), 1 dish

Simmered Celery, Kelp, and Carrot (page 182), 1 dish

Snappy Water Chestnut With Lotus Root Soup (page 72), 1 bowl

"Though family history is one of the causes, these diseases are often the result of disorderly and unbalanced life styles, especially in regards to food intake."

Heart Disease

The term heart disease can include arteriosclerosis, angina, myocardial infarction (heart attack), stroke, cardiomyopathy, congestive heart failure, heart-valve disease, and other ailments. Though family history is one of the causes, these diseases are often the result of disorderly and unbalanced life styles, especially in regards to food intake.

Arteriosclerosis, for example, is caused by a buildup of fatty deposits (plaque) inside the arteries. The plaque narrows the arteries causing either a decrease in the blood flow or a complete blockage. When this happens, the heart doesn't get the oxygen it needs.

People at the highest risk for this disease are those who are obese, smoke, have a sedentary lifestyle, have a family history of the disease, eat a high-fat diet, and/or have high cholesterol levels (over 230mg/dl). There is no treatment for arteriosclerosis, but if you exercise regularly, reduce the amount of fat in your diet, stop smoking, and lower your cholesterol, you will greatly reduce your risk of having a heart attack.

Master Hou's advice:

» Eat plain foods. Avoid greasy foods such as high fat meats.

» Avoid overeating at meal times.

» Vegetarian foods should dominate in your selections.

» Rice, wheat, fish, chicken, and lamb are proper foods for those suffering from heart disease. But don't let animal fat exceed 20% of your total caloric intake and 10% of your total fat intake. Avoid high-cholesterol foods like animal organs, egg yolks, shrimp, and lobster.

» Eat less processed foods like rice, wheat flour, and corn and avoid highly processed foods.

» Eat more fresh vegetables and fruits to lower blood fat and accelerate your metabolism.

» Do more exercises to improve the supply of blood to your heart muscle.

Suggested foods for heart disease:

Breakfast:
Oatmeal or grits, soy milk, juice, whole-wheat bread, fruit

Lunch:
Vegetables, salads, rice, fruit, seafood, chicken

Dinner:
Vegetables, fruit, tofu, soup, rice dishes, chicken, lamb

Diet plan for a week

Follow this diet plan for two months. You can vary the actual foods you choose by using this plan, and the other advice I have given you, as a general guideline. Corresponding page numbers are provided for the specific recipes that can be found in this book.

MONDAY

Breakfast

Soy milk, 1 glass

Sweet and Sour Cucumbers (page 165), 1 dish

Wheat bread, 1 slice

Lunch

Vegetable salad, 1 dish

Vegetable Rice Casserole (page 223), 1 dish

Dinner

Chinese Cabbage With Mushrooms (page 150), 1 dish

Pork Spareribs With Kelp Soup (page 54), 1 bowl

Fruit (an apple, orange, or banana), 1 piece

Steamed rice, 1 bowl

TUESDAY

Breakfast

Golden Fried Wheat Flour Tea (page 38), 1 glass

Orange juice, 1 glass

Fruit (an apple or a banana), 1 piece

Lunch

Steamed Spinach Noodles (page 228), 1 plate

Vegetable salad, 1 dish

Dinner

Tofu with Green Onions (page 171), 1 dish

Mushrooms With Garlic (page 154), 1 dish

Fruit (an orange, apple, banana, or kiwi), 1 piece

WEDNESDAY

Breakfast

Oatmeal or grits, 1 bowl

Fresh carrot juice, 1 dish

Lemon tea, 1 glass

Lunch

Spicy Gingered Chicken (page 106), 1 dish

Sandwich (chicken or tuna), 1 piece

Fruit (an orange, apple, banana, or kiwi), 1 cup

Dinner

Tomato and Pork Soup (page 69), 1 bowl

Beef With Snow Peas and Tofu (page 103, 1 dish

Steamed rice, 1 small bowl

THURSDAY

Breakfast

Soy milk plus an egg white, 1 glass

Cucumber With Coriander and Hot Green Pepper (page 167), 1 dish

Bread, 1 slice

Tea or black coffee, 1 cup

Lunch

White Rice Congee (page 220), 1 bowl

Scallop Fried Rice (page 222), 1 dish

Fruit (an orange, apple, banana, or kiwi), 1 piece

Dinner

Hot Green Pepper with Potato Strips (page 191), 1 dish

Spicy Gingered Chicken (page 106), 1 dish

Chinese Cabbage and Tofu Soup (page 73), 1 bowl

FRIDAY

Breakfast

Soy milk or White Rice Congee (page 220), 1 glass or 1 bowl

Simple Spiced-up Celery (page 172), 1 dish

Wheat bread, 1 slice

Chrysanthemum Tea (page 33) or green tea, 1 cup

Lunch

Sandwich (chicken or tuna), 1 sandwich

Vegetable salad, 1 dish

Fresh carrot juice, 1 glass

Dinner

Pork with Carrots (page 97), 1 dish

Mushrooms With Garlic (page 154), 1 dish

White or brown rice, or wheat bread, optional

Bamboo Shoots and Tofu Soup (page 48), 1 bowl

SATURDAY

Breakfast

Oatmeal or grits, 1 bowl
Simmered Celery, Kelp, and Carrot (page 182), 1 dish
Wheat bread, 1 slice

Lunch

Pork With Carrots (page 97), 1 dish
Fruit (an orange, apple, banana, or kiwi), 1 piece
Carrot juice, 1 glass

Dinner

Jellyfish and Turnip (page 140), 1 dish
Green Bell Pepper with Green Bean Sprouts (page 179), 1 dish
Soybean and Pork Spareribs Soup (page 66), 1 dish
Fruit, 1 piece

SUNDAY

Breakfast & lunch

Golden Fried Wheat Flour Tea (page 38), 1 dish
Fruit juice, 1 glass
Stewed Lamb Rice (page 224), 1 dish

Dinner

Tomato and Pork Soup (page 69), 1 bowl
Vegetable salad, 1 dish
Fish Fillet With Garlic and Ginger Cucumbers (page 136), 1 dish
Bread, 2 pieces

"Evidence points to a link between a high-fat diet and certain cancers, such as cancer of the breast, colon, uterus, and prostate. "

Cancer

Our current understanding of the causes of cancer is incomplete. Cancer develops gradually as a result of a complex mix of factors related to one's environment, lifestyle, and heredity.

There are many factors that are known to increase the risk of cancer, the most common of which are following:

Tobacco. Tobacco causes cancer. Tobacco use is the most preventable cause of death in this country. If you smoke, quit.

Diet. Your choice of foods may affect your risk of developing cancer. Evidence points to a link between a high-fat diet and certain cancers, such as cancer of the breast, colon, uterus, and prostate. Being seriously overweight appears to be linked to increased rates of cancer of the prostate, pancreas, uterus, colon, and ovaries, as well as breast cancer in older women.

Sunlight. Ultraviolet radiation from the sun and from other sources (such as sunlamps and tanning booths) damages the skin and can cause skin cancer.

Alcohol. Drinking large amounts of alcohol increases the risk of cancer of the mouth, throat, esophagus, and larynx. (People who smoke cigarettes and drink alcohol have an especially high risk of getting these cancers.) Alcohol can damage the liver and increase the risk of liver cancer. Some studies suggest that drinking alcohol also increases the risk of breast cancer. Drink alcohol only in moderation.

"Drinking large amounts of alcohol increases the risk of cancer of the mouth, throat, esophagus, and larynx."

Radiation. X-rays used for diagnosis expose you to very little radiation, and the benefits nearly always outweigh the risks. Repeated exposure, however, can be harmful, so it is a good idea to talk with your doctor or dentist about the need for each X-ray and ask about the use of shields to protect other parts of your body.

Chemicals and other substances in the workplace. Being exposed to substances like metals, dust, chemicals, or pesticides at work can increase the risk of cancer. Asbestos, nickel, cadmium, uranium, radon, vinyl chloride, benzidene, and benzene are other examples of carcinogens in the workplace.

"Try to have a varied, well-balanced diet that includes generous amounts of foods that are high in fiber, vitamins, and minerals, especially vegetables, fruits, and other plain (unprocessed) foods."

Master Hou's advice:

Cancer is a term used to describe a group of more than 100 different diseases. Here are some general guidelines to follow as preventive measures, and to help you regain your health if you do have cancer.

» Studies suggest that foods containing large amounts of fiber and certain nutrients help protect us against some types of cancer. You may be able to reduce your cancer risk by making some simple food choices. Try to have a varied, well-balanced diet that includes generous amounts of foods that are high in fiber, vitamins, and minerals, especially vegetables, fruits, and other plain (unprocessed) foods.

» Cut down on fatty foods. You should eat five servings of fruits and vegetables each day. Choose more whole-grain breads and cereals, and cut down on eggs, high-fat meat, high-fat dairy products (such as whole milk, butter, and most cheeses), salad dressings, margarine, and cooking oils.

» Eating well means getting enough calories and protein to help prevent weight loss and regain strength. Patients who eat well during cancer treatment often feel better and have more energy. In addition, they may be better able to handle the side effects of treatment.

» Do not drink alcohol. If you drink at all, do so in moderation—not more than one or two drinks a day.

» Quit smoking.

» Try to avoid pungent foods like ginger, garlic, hot pepper, chives, and some seafood like yellow fish, crab, and shrimp. These foods are believed to cause further deterioration.

» Try to eat organic foods. Many cancers may be the result of chemical substances in foods.

"Patients who eat well during cancer treatment often feel better and have more energy."

Diet plan for a week

Follow this diet plan for two months. You can vary the actual foods you choose by using this plan, and the other advice I have given you, as a general guideline. Corresponding page numbers are provided for the specific recipes that can be found in this book.

MONDAY

Breakfast

Soy milk plus nuts or seeds, 1 glass
Sweet and Sour Cucumbers (page 165), 1 dish
Whole grain bread, 1 slice

Lunch

Vegetable salad, 1 dish
Vegetable Rice Casserole (page 223), 1 dish

Dinner

Bitter Melon With Soybeans (page 162), 1 dish
Pork Spareribs With Kelp Soup (page 54), 1 bowl
Fruit (an apple, orange, or banana), 1 piece
Steamed rice, 1 bowl

TUESDAY

Breakfast

Golden Fried Wheat Flour Tea (page 38), 1 glass
Orange juice, 1 glass
Fruit (apple or banana), 1 piece

Lunch

Steamed Spinach Noodles (page 228), 1 plate
Vegetable salad, 1 dish

Dinner

Tofu with Minced Pork (page 94), 1 dish
Herbed Lamb Soup (page 57), 1 bowl
Steamed rice or wheat bread, 1 bowl/1 piece
Fruit (an orange, apple, banana, or kiwi), 1 piece

WEDNESDAY

Breakfast

Oatmeal or grits, 1 bowl
Fresh carrot juice, 1 dish

Lunch

Sandwich (chicken or tuna), 1 dish
Fruit (an orange, apple, banana, or kiwi), 1 piece

Dinner

Laver, Tofu, and Pork Soup (page 58), 1 bowl
Vegetable salad, 1 dish
Steamed rice, 1 bowl

THURSDAY

Breakfast

Soy milk plus one egg white, 1 glass
Bitter Melon With Soybeans (page 162), 1 dish
Whole grain bread, 1 slice

Lunch

White Rice Congee (page 220), 1 bowl
Vegetable Rice Casserole (page 223), 1 dish
Fruit (an orange, apple, banana, or kiwi), 1 piece

Dinner

Spicy Bite Radishes (page 195), 1 dish
Chinese Cabbage and Tofu Soup (page 73), 1 bowl
Steamed rice, 1 bowl

FRIDAY

Breakfast

Soy milk or White Rice Congee (page 220), 1 glass/1 bowl

Sesame Spinach (page 163), 1 dish

Wheat bread, 1 slice

Lunch

Sandwich (chicken or tuna), 1 piece

Vegetable salad, 1 dish

Fresh carrot juice, 1 glass

Dinner

Piquant Pork and Spinach (page 90), 1 dish

Peanuts and Celery (page 187), 1 dish

White rice, brown rice, or wheat bread, optional, 1 dish or 1 slice

Pork and Green-bean-sprouts Soup (page 88), 1 bowl

SATURDAY

Breakfast

Oatmeal or grits, 1 bowl

Cauliflower in Stewed Sauce (page 205), 1 dish

Wheat bread, 1 slice

Lunch

Vegetable Rice Casserole (page 223), 1 dish

Fruit (an orange, apple, banana, or kiwi), 1 piece

Carrot juice, 1 glass

Dinner

Bitter Melon With Soybeans (page 162), 1 dish

Tomato and Pork Soup (page 69), 1 bowl

Wheat bread, 1 slice

Fruit, 1 piece

SUNDAY

Breakfast and lunch

Golden Fried Wheat Flour Tea (page 38), 1 glass

Fruit juice, 1 glass

Stewed Lamb Rice (page 224), 1 dish

Dinner

Laver, Tofu, and Pork Soup (page 58), 1 bowl

Vegetable salad, 1 dish

Fish Fillet With Garlic and Ginger Cucumbers (page 136), 1 dish

Wheat bread or steamed rice, 2 pieces or 1 bowl

"Exercise, such as a daily walk or swim, helps keep joints moving, reduces pain, and strengthens muscles around the joints."

Arthritis

There are more than 100 different forms of arthritis and many different symptoms and treatments. We do not know what causes most forms of arthritis. Some forms are, however, better understood than others.

Arthritis causes pain and loss of movement and can affect joints in any part of the body. It is usually chronic, meaning it can occur over a long period of time. The more serious forms can cause excessive swelling, warmth, redness, and pain. The three most common kinds of arthritis in older people are osteoarthritis, rheumatoid arthritis, and gout.

People taking medicine for any form of arthritis should limit the amount of alcohol they drink.

Exercise, such as a daily walk or swim, helps keep joints moving, reduces pain, and strengthens muscles around the joints. Rest is also important for the joints affected by arthritis. Physical therapists can develop personal programs that balance exercise and rest.

Many people find that soaking in a warm bath, swimming in a heated pool, or applying heat or cold to the area around the joint helps reduce pain.

Controlling or losing weight can reduce the stress on joints and can help avoid further damage.

Master Hou's advice:

Osteoarthritis

- Regular moderate physical activities are advised to help strengthen bone and muscles. Good ones to try are bike riding or swimming in warm water.
- If you are overweight, try to lose weight to reduce the stress on joints.
- Do not remain sedentary. Get up and move around if you are sitting at a desk. Take frequent breaks if you are driving long distances.

Rheumatoid Arthritis

Scientists don't know what causes Rheumatoid Arthritis (RA). Researchers theorize that it has something to do with a breakdown in the immune system, the body's defense against disease. It is also likely that people who get RA have certain inherited traits (genes) that cause a disturbance in the immune system.

- There are no effective ways to prevent or cure RA at this time.

"Although I cannot recommend a specific diet plan for arthritis, a number of my recipes do help to relieve symptoms such as painful and swollen joints."

» An alcoholic drink can relieve some of the symptoms. The key is moderation. In China, people drink "herb wine" to treat RA.

Gout

» Keep body weight down, but do not fast because it may cause more uric acid to accumulate.

» Do not drink alcohol, especially beer. If drinking at all, men should limit themselves to two small glasses and women to one glass.

» Avoid foods with large amounts of protein, such as animal organs, seafood, or beans.

Unlike the other diseases I specifically discussed in this appendix, arthritis is not as directly related to food intake. The individual characteristics of the specific diseases found under the arthritis umbrella are so different that it is difficult to create a diet plan that would work for all of them. Arranging a diet based on the guidelines given above, while cooperating positively with your doctor is the best solution.

Although I cannot recommend a specific diet plan for arthritis, a number of my recipes do help to relieve symptoms such as painful and swollen joints. Try several and see which ones work best for you.

APPENDIX IV

The Nature of Common Foods

As discussed in Chapter 2, *An Introduction to Traditional Chinese Medicine* all foods can be categorized according to their nature. With this knowledge we can design our diet around our body types; eating the specific kinds of foods that our body type requires to remain balanced and healthy. Below you will find some helpful charts outlining the nature of some foods that are commonly found in Asian cooking.

Foods with Cool or Cold Natures

Apple	Cucumber	Lily bulb	Soy sauce
Bamboo shoot	Lotus root	Spinach	Banana
Duck meat	Millet	Sponge gourd	Barley
Eggplant	Mung bean	Tomato	Bitter melon
Frog meat	Oranges	Turnip (white)	Buckwheat
Green cabbage	Oyster	Watermelon	Celery

Foods with Cool or Cold Natures, continued

Green tea	Pear	Winter melon	Coix seed
Kelp	Salt	Crystal sugar	
Laver (seaweed)	Crab	Lettuce	

Foods with Warm or Hot Natures

Apricot	Coriander	Longan	Black tea
Mustard green	Brown sugar	Mutton	Sorghum
Chestnut	Fennel	Onion	Trout
Cherry	Garlic	Peach	Turkey
Chicken	Ginger	Pepper	Vinegar
Chinese date	Rice	Pineapple	Walnut
Chives	Carp	Plum	Wine
Coffee	Hot pepper	Pomegranate	

Foods with Neutral or Plain Natures

Abalone	Mushroom	Quail meat	Beef Eel
Olive	Red bean	Cabbage	Goose meat
Oolong tea	Rice	Carp	Grape
Pea	Soybean	Carrot	Honey
Peanut	Cauliflower	Jasmine tea	Sugar (white)
Jellyfish	Pork	Turtle	Chinese yam
Lemon	Potato	Wheat	Corn
Lotus seed	Yellow croaker		

Resources

The ingredients I have used in these recipes are common in China. I carefully selected each because of their medicinal value. Some ingredients however, may seem a little exotic to the average reader. As you prepare to make some of these dishes you may find yourself wondering where to find some of the ingredients.

The simplest and quickest way to find the items on your Chinese food shopping list is to visit the nearest Asian grocery store. Most towns have at least one Asian food market. Many larger cities have a Chinatown district you can visit which will have a number of grocery stores to choose from. Because of the similarity in Chinese, Japanese, Korean, and Filipino cuisines any Asian market should have most of the ingredients you are looking for. Indian food markets are a good place to check for some of the ingredients as well. You might also be pleasantly surprised by how many of the ingredients you can find in your mainstream and natural food stores as well.

"The simplest and quickest way to find the items on your Chinese food shopping list is to visit the nearest Asian grocery store. Most towns have at least one Asian food market."

If you are having trouble locating an Asian grocery store in your town, or you prefer the convenience of online shopping, please take a look at the following online resources. Several of the resources listed also have information on Asian cooking equipment including steamers and woks.

EthnicGrocer.com

Website: www.ethnicgrocer.com

Phone: 1-866-438-4642

This is an easy to use and extensive site of reasonably priced ethnic foods and products. Choose the "groceries" link from the pull-down menu for a larger number of choices.

AsiaFoods.com

Website: www.asiafoods.com

Phone: 1-877-902-0841

This is a comprehensive Asian supply site including everything from fruits and vegetables to bamboo steamers. If your looking for a hard to find Asian food item your likely to locate it here.

The Oriental Pantry

Website: www.orientalpantry.com

Phone: (978) 264-4576

Fax: (781) 275-4506

Address: The Oriental Pantry
423 Great Road (2A)
Acton, MA 01720

This is an excellent Asian grocery site with a large selection, including many hard to find items.

CTCFood.com

Website: www.ctcfood.com

Phone: 1-800-356-3134 ext. 7493 or (650) 292-7493

Fax: (650) 871-9154

Address: CTC Food
131 West Harris Avenue
South San Francisco, CA 94080

This site features quality Asian foods at competitive prices. The wide variety of items they carry include tofu, sesame oil, canned lychee fruit, water chestnuts, and dried mushrooms.

Pacificrim-gourmet.com

Website: www.pacificrim-gourmet.com

Phone: 1-800-910-9657 or (858) 274-9013

Fax: (858) 274-9018

Address: i-Clipse, Inc.
4905 Morena Boulevard, Suite 1313
San Diego, CA 92117

This site features Asian-cooking equipment including woks, rice cookers, steamers, spices, and other ingredients.

iKoreaplaza

Website: www.ikoreaplaza.com

Phone: (510) 238-8940

Address: iKoreaplaza
2370 Telegraph Avenue
Oakland, CA 94612

This online Korean supermarket carries items you might find on your list including sesame seeds, rice, noodles, produce, and beans.

Index

Index By Chapter

Beverages

Soups

Meat

Poultry

Seafood

Seafood, continued

Vegetarian

Vegetarian , continued

Vegetarian , continued

Rice and Noodles

Rice and Noodles, *continued*

Desserts

NOTES

NOTES

NOTES

NOTES

NOTES

NOTES

NOTES

NOTES